This book is a publication of
Indiana University Press
601 North Morton Street
Bloomington, Indiana 47404-3797 USA

www.indiana.edu/~iupress

Telephone orders 800-842-6796
Fax orders 812-855-7931
Orders by e-mail iuporder@indiana.edu

The paper used in this publication meets the minimum
requirements of American National Standard for Information
Sciences—Permanence of Paper for Printed Library
Materials, ANSI Z39.48-1984.

Manufactured in the United States of America

Library of Congress Cataloging-in-Publication Data

Logsdon, Gene.
     You can go home again : adventures of a contrary life /
Gene Logsdon
        p.   cm.
     ISBN 0-253-33419-5 (alk. paper). —
     ISBN 0-253-21218-9 (pbk. : alk. paper)
     1. Logsdon, Gene. 2. Ohio—Social life and customs. 3.
Farm life—Ohio. 4. Ohio—Biography.   I. Title.
F496.2.L64 1998
977.1'043'092—dc21
[B]   98-17125
1 2 3 4 5 03 02 01 00 99 98

For Joe Dan Boyd, who did it too

Contents

Preface

It was not until I was fifty-five years old that I realized that my life had followed roads so less traveled by that even Robert Frost might have shaken his head in doubt and wonder. I was at first embarrassed by this realization because I understood for the first time how stupidly naive I must appear to smart people who had spent their first fifty-five years getting rich. Then I realized that my life really was unique (beyond being uniquely naive) and that even from a historical point of view, my experiences might be worth writing down—as a kind of droll, sad hymn to the passing of rural culture.

I grew up on a farm in the '30s and '40s, in the embrace of an agrarian society that was closer to the latter nineteenth century than to the world I would have to cope with in the latter twentieth, condemning me to march out of step all the days of my adult life. I belonged to the last generation of that old rural society that dominated America's value system (whatever that is) until about 1955. I witnessed the dying-down days of a farming culture that had really not changed much since the invention of the scythe, the reaping hook, and the three divine persons in one God. To accentuate the sense of loss and death that my accident of birth thrust upon me, I spent ten years in Catholic seminaries where I witnessed the last days of the old monastic lifestyle too. Until I was twenty-four, my life was in a time warp.

Not having suffered enough, I decided that my future lay in big-time farming. Our family "geared up" (the verb so beloved by agribusiness journalists) to milk a hundred cows. If suffering and poverty could make a Writer, I would have become a new Steinbeck. But all I learned from a hundred cows was how wise the old farm ways had been and how insane were the new ways.

I moved then, not by any plan but by simply stumbling along, into what is so euphorically called "higher" education, thinking innocently that what the death of rural tradition and monastic life plus my own contrariness prohibited me from doing, I could do as a Professor of Air-Tight Financial Security. Failing that, I wandered on, in desperation, into journalism, thinking with championship-brand naivete that as a writer I could "do good in the world." I found that I was as willing as any journalist to write for money now and worry about the effects of what I wrote later. Disillusioned, I quit a good job, forced by the fact of my blunders to realize that only by going home, physically and spiritually, was I ever going to achieve what I called success, which for me was mostly the opposite of how modernity defined that word.

The uniqueness of my life lies not so much in any one area of achievement, or in my case, failure, but in my strange combination of failures. Is there anyone else in the world who has experienced intimately both nineteenth- and twentieth-century farming, the monk-like ordeals of a seminarian studying for the priesthood, the earnest pomposities of postgraduate studies in the liberal arts, and the Henny Penny cluckings of magazine journalism? Is there anyone else in all the universe who today comes in from birthing a lamb and sits down to a word processor to report on the environmental travails of trying to dispose of millions of disposable diapers?

All that takes place in this book really did happen, and I'm sorry about that. I have used only nicknames or first names where I thought personal privacy was in order, and a couple of times I relied on a composite of more than one incident to keep the narrative flowing along without undue detail. But in no case has any important truth in the matter been violated. If I erred, it was because thirty to fifty years, or even two weeks, is a long time to remember accurately, even for someone like myself who is cursed with a mind that never forgets certain kinds of trivial details. I'm sure my mind erred unwittingly in other trivial details, and that the errors were not caught by readers familiar with my past, who are bigger exaggerators than I am anyway. In all important ways, this book is true. I hope it gives encouragement to others who are wandering through life looking for home or wondering if there is such a thing as a true home. Believe me, there is. Just go contrary into the world and you can find it.

Acknowledgments

John Gallman of Indiana University Press has been of immense help not only in editing this manuscript but in giving invaluable advice about the writing and in inspiring me by his own homestead work. Richard Gilbert at Ohio University Press, who shares my vision of an America of garden farms, gave great encouragement and inspiration also. Parts of some of the essays in this book appeared originally in *Ohio* magazine; the *Country Journal*; the *Farm Journal*; *Plain* magazine; and an anthology, *The Earth at Our Doorstep*, from Sierra Club Books. I also thank the editors involved, especially John Baskin, Jean Kelly, Joe Dan Boyd, Jerry Carlson, Gertrude Dieken, Richard Ketcham, Tyler Resch, Peter Fossel, Scott Savage, and Annie Stine.

You
Can Go
Home
Again

CHAPTER 1 / *Homesick*

I glared across the serving counter into the school kitchen, past the platters of fried bitch and bowls of hemorrhage that the nuns were dishing up for us, my attention riveting on the pies. I took note of the T-bone steaks and the mashed potatoes and the baby bibb lettuce headed for the priests' refectory, but it was the cherry pies, the red juice oozing around the edges of the top crust, that caught my eye and pushed me over the edge. After three and a half years in the high school prep-seminary at Mount Saint Francis, Indiana, where I had gone to begin studies for the priesthood, I was fed up, literally, at seeing the good food going to the priests who taught us, while we ate boarding-school crap. The fried bitch, our name for baloney, was okay, actually, unless you ate seventeen sandwiches of it at one meal like Herm did and had to have your stomach pumped out because of all that grease and white bread balling up in your belly. I kind of liked the greaseburgers that the nuns were famous for too, although not as well as White Castles, which we savored on Christmas and Easter, when, desperately homesick and not allowed to go home, we roamed the dismal streets of Louisville, Kentucky. But the reddish, runny stuff we called hemorrhage got tiresome in a hurry, let alone over a span of nearly four school years. So did the shoe leather that passed for roast beef, the canned baked beans that acquired taste only after inundation with ketchup, and the hardboiled potatoes whose only grace was to act as an effective sop under the baked beans and hemorrhage. Our desserts were tin-canned peaches, plums, and the ever present applesauce that tasted like wet, slightly sweetened sawdust. My friend and classmate Bee maintained that most of our food was Army surplus left over from the war and since America beat the Germans and the Japs on it, it must not be too bad.

But by God I was going to have one of those homemade pies that the faculty enjoyed every week, even if I had to steal it, which I most certainly would have to do. The pies appeared to be the equal of the ones Mom made at home if that were possible. The smell and the flaky texture of the dough said lard crust to me, and the pies looked more enticing, sitting there all in a row on the cooling shelf above the huge institutional oven, than a line of beauty queens sitting on a diving board. We had tried on many occasions to sweet-talk the German nuns, especially the younger one who smiled occasionally, into secretly passing us dessert morsels from the priests' table. But the young nun only laughed nervously and kept saying "shuss mi-noots," which stood for "just a minute," the only English words she didn't know, and the nuns' standard answer to our constant, imploring question, How long till we eat? We ate at the same times every day of course—7:30 A.M., 12:00 noon, and 6:00 P.M. I often wondered how the nuns stood such a life so far from their homeland, cloistered from any outside contacts by language and way of life, working every day for nine months of the year cooking and doing the laundry for seventy rowdy boys who ate like hogs, and all year for at least twelve priests. Being away from home for just nine months at a time was hard enough. I wondered what it must be like for them. What a vision of God nuns must have.

Stealing a pie out of the kitchen turned out to be more difficult than it at first appeared. The kitchen was off limits to us, and both regular entrances were in almost constant view of someone in authority. There was at least one nun in the kitchen all day long, and at night, slipping out of the dormitory, past the rooms of Father Hilary, the Prefect, and Father Nicholas, the Assistant Prefect, was extremely risky. I had never tried such a stunt in all the time I had been in boarding school, and the idea of doing so now filled me with apprehension. Hilary could smell mischief a mile away. There was the Rector, Father Vincent, to watch out for, too, roaming around at all hours of the day and night, paranoid as hell about students doing something stupid. Not without reason. Bee and I once almost burned the chapel down when a fire started accidentally in our photographic darkroom in the movie projection room under the church. (I don't think Vince, who called our class the worst in seminary history, was ever fully convinced that it was an accident.) Also to be considered, if a raid on the kitchen were made in daylight, was Father Albert in the post office with nothing better to do during the day than watch out the windows, which looked directly onto the kitchen. Then there was Father Norbert, the Procurator, who came in and out of the kitchen regularly, checking on food supplies to see what he needed to buy. Always eyes, wittingly or otherwise, watching our every move. And if not, some little pipsqueak of a freshman or sophomore, seeking favor, might squeal on us.

"Bee, I want one of those pies."

"Who doesn't?"

"I mean I want one of those pies real bad."

"So?"

"Got any ideas?"

We pondered the problem. Though the door between the storeroom and the boilerroom, to which we had access, was usually locked, it suggested a possibility. We might slip the pies out through that door unnoticed and hide them in the boilerroom until we could smuggle them to our hideout in the woods.

"I got it," Clutch said, snapping his fingers. We had brought him into the scheme along with Screwball because they could be trusted and four heads were better than two. "Why don't we just make the raid during the basketball game Friday night when everybody will be in the gym and lots of outsiders will be in the building. Friday is also bake day in the kitchen."

"And when the pies come up missing, maybe Hilary will blame an outsider," Screwball reasoned hopefully.

But there was a hitch to this plan. I was on the basketball team, and so unavailable for raiding kitchens at that time.

"That settles it," I said to no one in particular.

"Settles what?" asked Bee.

"I've been wanting to quit basketball anyway, and now I will. I just got too much else to do." I spent most of the game time on the bench, which made the idea of quitting the team a little more appealing.

At an opportune moment, I screwed up my courage and went to Hilary's office. He was a kindly man and a good basketball coach. I felt guilty about what I was about to tell him.

"What can I do for you, Henry?" he asked cheerfully. Calling me by my middle name was his little joke.

"Father, I've decided to quit the basketball team."

His face fell. After what seemed a long time he answered. "I wish you wouldn't. We've got such few players. The team needs a good bench."

I did not reply, so he continued. "I'd like to play you more. Your offense is good, but your defense just isn't up there yet with the first-stringers."

"Oh, it's not that," I replied quickly, although of course it was, at least partially. "I just have taken on too many extracurricular activities working in the wood shop, the darkroom, and especially writing for and putting out the school paper." I did not mention roaming the several hundred acres of woods and fields around the seminary, my first priority. "I just have to give up something and basketball seems to be the best choice."

"You know that quitting anything you've committed yourself to is not a sign of good character," he said, as gently as he could.

"I have to quit something and it might as well be something

I'm least cut out for," I said, almost holding my breath by now.

He looked out the window and sighed. Finally he said, "Well, if you change your mind, don't be afraid to say so."

I went back to my desk, a little surprised at how easy the encounter had gone off. Then a new feeling flowed through me. For the first time in my life I had made a decision all on my own, not to please anyone: not a parent, not a teacher, not a priest, not even myself, since I liked to play sports. A feeling of cool self-confidence swept over me and it felt good. My mind, that wayward spirit I could never control, embraced the confidence and leaped ahead of it. *Why could I not make the same kind of realistic decision to quit the seminary?* Immediately I clamped off that train of thought. Questioning the will of God was sinful. Better to concentrate on stealing pies.

The kitchen doors would be locked on game night for sure. Somehow we needed to get inside the storeroom ahead of time to unlock the boilerroom door. By coincidence, late Friday afternoon was the time that the Procurator always brought in a big load of groceries to replenish the kitchen storeroom. We could be lolling outside in the vicinity of the kitchen door at this time after classes without drawing suspicion. We could offer to help Norb carry the boxes of food into the storeroom. Someone would, at a precise instant when neither Norb nor any nun was watching, release the mechanism that made the boilerroom door lock automatically from the inside. If the nuns did not look closely, they would not realize that the door was unlocked and we could slip in through the boilerroom during the game and grab the pies.

I couldn't sleep the night before the raid. Three times I decided not to go through with it. Four times, I changed my mind. Lying in bed, I did what I did whenever the present was more than I could handle: I slipped into my file of memories and imagined myself at home. I had never really wanted to go away to school, having done so for the same reason my uncles went to war. It was my duty. God had called me to His army, to war against evil. Or so I was taught and so I believed. But my mind wouldn't cooperate with my belief. It stayed home, living over and over those years of boyhood and high school summers on the farm. My inner self viewed the time at school as a theatrical performance in which I had to act a part until the curtain fell and I could go back home again.

The dormitory darkness faded away into a sunny October day. I saw myself, faraway and nine years old, riding Flora, who was pulling the corn binder with our other workhorse, Bell, while Mom, in the iron seat of the binder, held the reins and guided the horses down the standing rows of corn. I was feeling extra good since I had just found an unbroken arrowhead on the bare ground of the corn field. My sister, Marilyn, a year younger, was trying her best to wheedle me into telling the exact spot where it had lain, as if arrowheads generated more arrowheads like mushrooms. But of course I wouldn't tell, so she was now sulking in one of the corn shocks, which we made-believe were Indian tepees, making corncob dolls with my other sister, Kak. My brother, Giles, born only three weeks earlier, lay asleep in a Friemann's wooden beer case bolted to the binder tongue. He slept better there with the bounce and clamor of the binder than he did in his quiet crib back home. Mom was singing my favorite song at the top of her voice, though the clattering sounds of the binder and the waywardness of the horses sometimes interrupted her.

> Climb upon my knee, sonny boy,
> —*Florie, get your lazy butt up there*—
> Though you're only three . . .
> (Clatter-dee-clat, thuhlactadee-clat-clat)
> . . . no way of knowing, and there's— *Florie!*
> What you mean to me, sonny . . .
> (Clatter-dee-clat, thuhlactadee-clat-clat)

When the binder carriage filled with bundles of corn, she would trip the little pedal that activated the conveyer chain with her heel. With a clatter-dee-clat, thuhlactadee-clat-clat, the conveyer rolled the bundles out on the ground beside the ones from the last pass across the field. Dad, meanwhile, went from one collection of bundles to another, setting them up in shocks, turning the field into a bucolic picture of peace and plenty. Whenever we passed him, I waved as if I had not seen him for days and he paused in his work and watched us go by with a tremendous satisfaction I could sense but had no word for.

Along about the middle of the afternoon, the October day grown hot and tempers grown short, the binder suddenly screeched with a new kind of noise. Mom whoaed the horses. The right gathering chain had broken.

"Shit," she said, wiping the sweat from her face. She was more worried about the sudden quiet waking the baby than about the broken machine.

Dad sauntered over and inspected the damage.

"Shit."

"That's what *I* said," Mom countered.

"Well, damn, then." Dad.

"Damn and shit." Mom.

"Well, damn, shit, and hell." Dad.

Mom giggled. "A hundred damns, shits, and hells."

"Ten thousand damns, shits, and hells!" By now they were both laughing, too tired to do anything else.

A deep, stentorian clearing of voice filled the air, as the new pastor of our church, Father McKeoun, out on his pastoral visits, stepped into view from the standing corn. He had evidently heard it all as he approached. Dad disappeared under the cogs and chains of the binder, and Mom wilted in her seat like a frosted tomato vine. I was the only one who saw the broad grin that spread momentarily over the priest's face.

The dormitory blackness closed in again. I slept in peace.

Friday morning. Chapel at 6:00. Breakfast, 7:30. Housekeeping. Class. Study hall. Class again. Study hall again. The minutes crawled by. At my study hall desk, I fidgeted in apprehension and anticipation. I had been a rather model student for three years, a born sucker for all the approval and recognition my good conduct heaped upon me. Now I was going to break a major rule. Something had come over me as a senior. It wasn't homemade pies either, I knew, but that damned Martin Luther. Running into Martin Luther in a Catholic prep-seminary was the kind of weird luck that seemed to dog my steps. Luther had become for me a source of gnawing doubt about religion and about myself that I could not overcome. Maybe today would be different. I needed something to take my mind off the coming heist anyway. I lifted my study hall desk lid and brought out a book titled *Luther*. Though a library book, I had checked it out so often that I finally decided just to keep it in my desk so the librarian would not get suspicious. The book discussed what the Church considered to be Luther's dreadful errors. It was so dull that I was sure no one else in school had ever tried to read it. I looked around, making sure students in nearby desks were not paying particular attention to me, as if there were pictures of naked women in the book. I flipped to the dog-eared page and read for at least the hundredth time the passage that was triggering my moral decline.

> Martin Luther might have weathered the storm over his denunciation of the Church's practice of granting indulgences, which had in truth fallen into abuse, but he succumbed to a much deeper error. He began to question the doctrine of Transubstantiation, the changing of the bread and wine into the body and blood of Christ during the Eucharistic Service, which doctrine is at the very core of Catholic theology. He decided that when Christ at the Last Supper said: "This is My Body" and "This is My Blood," He did not mean the phrases literally, as the Church teaches, but symbolically. Luther, having reached that conclusion, staunchly maintained it against all accusation of heresy.

I closed the book and shivered. I could pretend to deny it, but it seemed to me that Luther was right. His explanation was tons more sensible than believing that a piece of bread *actually* changed into the body of Christ while retaining the appearance of bread, as Catholicism taught. Why tout a miracle when none was needed? I could no more dispel my conviction that Luther's explanation was the better of the two than I could deny that two plus two equaled four. That was dire enough heresy, but if two plus two equaled four in this regard, then eight plus eight equaled sixteen—that is to say, much of the Church's other doctrinal teachings were probably wrong too. Oh God. I was a heretic going straight to hell, right here in a Catholic school. I looked around. No one was watching me, no one could hear my heart thumping, my mind screaming out in frustration.

I proceeded through the same angst-ridden line of reasoning that I always followed to escape the anguish of my predicament. What was I to do? My teachers, who told me I was smart and talented as a writer and headed for a glorious career in the service of the Church (how I ate that up), would reject me if they knew. I would be kicked out of school. I couldn't even ask them about my doubts without revealing my dirty little heretical secret. Holy Mother the Church, from whom all blessings flowed, in whom my salvation, earthly and heavenly, was irretrievably entwined, was a theological house of cards, a mirage of doctrinal make-believe. But what could I do but play along? Where could I turn? How could I strike out on my own? I didn't even have enough money to buy myself a sack of White Castles. If I left the seminary, I would not escape my heretical leprosy. My parents, who were steadfast Catholics, would disown me too. I had to stay put until I figured out a solution. My only defense was the religious one I had been trained to take. As with thinking about sex, thinking heresy was sinful, and such thoughts had to be ruthlessly banished from my mind. I couldn't banish either subject, of course. But I could replace them by thinking about stealing pies.

I wondered if I was sick in the head. Maybe Catholic doctrine appeared wrong to me but to none of the other people I knew because I was literally insane. I remembered my grade school years, which provided evidence for such a fear. How could I have been so naive as to allow dear Sister Monica to talk me into going to the prep-seminary so far from home? I thought I knew the answer although I was afraid to admit it. Not only did I crave her approval, having a crush on her, but I loved the instant recognition I received in school and at home when I announced that I had decided to study for the priesthood. My parents, busy caring for a house full of younger siblings and a barn full of animals, had previously all but ignored me. I was somebody special now. Even though they thought I was too young to leave home, they acceded to the priests who said it was God's will and no one dared stand in the way. Grandmaw pointed out that it must be God's will because I got good grades in school, a sure sign that I was supposed to be a priest. Marilyn, my sister, was the only one in the family who disagreed. "Farmers are smarter than priests," she said, defying me to argue with her. When her teachers told her she would make a good nun, she snorted and said she wanted to make babies. "You a priest?" she said to me with a laugh. "You must be nuts."

A whisper from Rafe at the desk next to me broke my reverie. "Hey. Come to. Time for history class."

After lunch, another study hall. I leafed through the calendar pad on my desk. Since January I had kept a countdown of the days till the heavenly arrival of summer vacation. Now, March 10, I wrote "77" beside the date. Seventy-seven more days till Paradise Regained.

I kept my favorite letters from home in a special packet, to be read again and again when the homesickness got me down. I pulled them out of my desk now and picked one of Dad's to read. I knew it by heart, but preferred to read his scrawly handwriting. The letter told about opening night of the trapping season, when he had caught fifty-four muskrats, two mink, and four raccoons. How I longed to have been there with him, having what was one of the most exciting adventures when I had been home. He went on to tell how he had fallen through thin ice and had to fight his way to the river bank. In fear of freezing to death, "I sort of played Daniel Boone, lit a fire, stripped off my clothes and held them over the fire with a stick till they were about dry. The fire did a pretty good job of keeping me warm in the meantime. Worked out better than I thought it would and I didn't even catch a cold."

Marilyn's letters always began or ended with "Boy, did we have fun." I figured she was trying to tempt me to quit school and come home. Many years later I would learn that she was nearly heart-broken when I went away. I picked the one now that she had sent two years ago, an account of Halloween night, when she took all the younger siblings on a walk through the woods, which she had convinced them was full of ghosts, and then sat around a bonfire in the barnyard telling stories and exploding buckeyes in the fire. Not a really momentous event, but she had sent along a photo of them all around the fire and that picture had the power to suck all the life out of me and fill the empty space with a bleak and ener-vating depression. When I was out in the woods in my secret place, I would often stare at the picture until I cried. Now, a hardheart-ed senior and a heretic, and soon to be a thief, I just stared at the picture in a kind of despair.

Mom's letters told, in a matter-of-fact way, of the farm's prog-ress through the seasons: fall harvest, winter barn chores, cozy nights eating popcorn and reading books, spring planting. Between the lines was always the clear message: how satisfied she was to be a farmer, no matter how hard the work or meager the income. I read one of her letters now from the preceding fall, when the whole family, except me of course, spent the day gathering hickory nuts and picnicking in the woods. Why couldn't I be there too? Why did I have to be the unlucky one God picked for his service? I thought of the homesick letters my cousin Bernard sent home from the army, as he yearned for the farm. But he would only be away for three years. I was going away forever.

Thinking of Bernard always brought to my mind my first bout of religious confusion. Slipping into the world of the past again, I was now six years old, walking home down the highway from school with my cousins, a dozen of us, looking as forlorn as a prison road gang. Normally we would have been riding the public school bus, but we had been unexpectedly banned from it because we went to Catholic school. Nothing in my childhood frame of refer-ence made room for the possibility or plausibility of this banning.

The other kids on the bus had never said they were not Catholics, or that there was something wrong with being one. As I walked along, I tried to think of a *reason* we were bad enough to be excluded. Unable to find one, even drawing upon the wildest excesses of my imagination, I rejected the ban as hearsay. Just some misunderstanding. Our bus driver was always nice to us, and when he passed on the road, as he soon would, he would stop and pick us up.

I kept looking back, watching for the bus to come into view. Up until the last second, I expected it to stop. I smiled and waved at my friend the driver. He never looked once at me, only stared stolidly ahead as he roared by, while children's shouts of Catlicker! Rednecker! Mackerel Snapper!—words I had never heard before—trailed out with the exhaust fumes behind the speeding bus. Those shouts and the set jaw of the driver still lay burning in my mind. I remembered the exact spot where I stood along Rt. 67 when the bus passed, at the curve where the Harpster road veers off to the left and my distrust in humankind veered off into my own peculiar world of elitist disdain.

"Why are they doing this?" I asked Bernard, the oldest cousin.

"Because we're Catholics."

"What are they?"

"Protestants."

"Prod-us-dunce." It was a new word. "What did we do to make them mad at us?"

"Nothing. When you have the true religion, expect to be persecuted, Sister says." He paused, and then added with evident relish. "They're all going to hell anyway."

The ban did not last long. Dad and my uncles raised holy hallelujah, something that they were very good at. "We pay taxes, by God, and by God we'll ride the buses!" I could still hear Uncle Lawrence thunder their battle cry. Soon we were back on the bus, and in later years, when I would ask about the incident, everyone pretended that it had not occurred.

The bell rang, jarring me back to the present. Study hall over. "Time for the great kitchen robbery to begin," Clutch whispered with great relish.

We stationed ourselves on the steps outside study hall, near the kitchen door, smoking our pipes—we weren't allowed cigarettes—waiting, trying to appear casual. The whole student body was alive with tension over the coming game with Borden that night, and so if Hilary had detected any unusual nervousness in our manner, he would attribute it to basketball jitters, we hoped. Right on time, Norbert pulled up in the school station wagon with his load of food. We sauntered over and greeted him as he pulled down the back door. Norb taught physics and chemistry and seemed forever mystified that we did not find chemical formulas as fascinating as he did.

"Can we help unload?" Bee asked. He could look more angelic than I. When I tried, I just looked suspicious.

Norb stared at us, hesitated at this show of student concern, then smiled and said, "Sure." Science was no help in predicting teenagers, and he didn't want to try anyway.

All four of us leaped eagerly to his aid, along with several other students who had no idea what we were up to, which made me want to burst into laughter. We grabbed boxes of food and followed Norbert through the kitchen door, briskly passed Sister Shuss-mi-noots, who was watching us curiously, and into the storeroom, where on a long table in the center of the room sat the pies. Oh my God. Norbert stood in the doorway between kitchen and storeroom, directing traffic. I slid my huge box, which happened to contain almost a whole stalk of bananas, onto the shelf where he indicated, then waited for my cohorts to crowd in with their boxes, shielding me a little from view as I drifted over to the boilerroom door. When Norb was looking back toward the kitchen, I released the lock. Over the edge I went.

Game time. In the balcony above the playing floor with the other students, I watched, feeling a twinge of regret as the players ran out onto the floor. I should have been with them. But my new sense of self-confidence at having quit the team overrode the regret. It might have been a dumb decision, but it was all mine.

Borden was supposed to overwhelm our little school, but the score see-sawed back and forth, keeping the spectators at fever pitch.

"Looks like a good time to do it," I said to my comrades, growing more apprehensive with each passing moment. We slipped out of the gym unnoticed in the pandemonium of cheering. No one was in the hall outside, and we quickly vanished into the boiler-room. Clutch quietly tried the knob on the door into the store-room. Sure enough, it was still unlocked. There was just enough light filtering through the windows from the outside pole lamp to guide us to the center table. I stared and groped in disbelief. The pies were gone!

I was almost relieved. I could get out of this dumb idea without losing face. We'd done our best, only to be outfoxed.

"Damn," Clutch whispered. We started giggling. With a rush we headed back out the door. But Screwball stopped suddenly, spying the bananas I had brought in earlier. The floodwaters of temptation having been let loose upon him, he was now not to be denied. He grabbed the whole stalk and bolted out the boilerroom door. We all followed. But in the instant after I passed, last, out the door, I remembered. I needed to release the mechanism that would lock the door behind us, covering our tracks. I stuck my head back through the door, snapped the lock release, and closed the door all in one motion. Standing in the boilerroom again, I had a sudden sickening consciousness of an image in my mind's eye, the silhouette of a nun standing in the doorway between the kitchen and the storeroom, silently staring at me as I locked the door. It had been only a fleeting glance, and I was not sure if the picture of it in my mind was real or imagined. But now was no time to stop and wonder. Clutch opened the door out of the boil-erroom. The coast was clear. We dashed across the hall and out the nearest exit into the darkness outside, Screwball bearing his stalk of bananas over his shoulder like a sack of potatoes, all of us running, giggling, on into the woods behind the tennis courts to our secret tree safe. We had lined a large hole in the bottom of a hollow beech with flattened tin cans, and added a door on the front to keep wild animals from getting food we received from home or contraband cigarettes we cached there. The stalk did not fit into the tree. We had to strip off the bananas and stack them. Then we raced back to the building, into the gym, and disappeared among the other students screaming in the balcony. No one had noticed our absence. Mission accomplished. We were winning the game.

Next day Vince, hot as a greaseburger just out of the skillet, came into the refectory as we were preparing to eat. He intended to find out who stole the bananas before any food was served. He would starve us into confession. No one volunteered anything, of course. No one knew anything except the four of us, and we were prepared to die before confessing. Even if they had, the tradition of the seminary decreed that anyone who squealed risked a "red belly," in which the hapless squealer was held on the ground on his back, his shirt pulled up, and his bare skin submitted to a steady, vigorous slapping until his stomach burned like fire and he finally vomited. Vince, knowing nothing of the horror of red bellies, roared, stomped, fumed, and threatened to withhold recreation for everyone until he was given a name. Seventy boys sat like stones in their chairs, hungrily eyeing the fried bitch growing cold on the countertop. Whatever punishment Vince would mete out could be borne because only seventy-six days remained until Paradise Regained. When I looked toward the food waiting tantalizingly for us, I saw Sister Shuss-mi-noots staring out at me from the kitchen with a very un-nunlike hint of a smile on her face. My God, she knows, I realized. She probably was on to us all along and that's why the pies had vanished. Son of a bitch. But she's not telling. Oh my God, what wonders Thou dost create.

Finally, in a purple rage, Vince stomped out of the refectory. The food was served. The idea of starving students into submission would not look good on provincial records. But we spent our recreation periods for five days in study hall.

"Habeas corpus," said the note Bee passed to me in study hall. I looked at him. What the hell does that mean?

Another note. "Vince has no body so he can't prove a murder."

Eventually, Vince decided no one would be dumb enough to steal a whole stalk of bananas and that the carry-out boys at the store had simply forgotten to put them in the station wagon. Sister Shuss-mi-noots continued to stare at us with an angelic smile. That spring we did not, as in other years, let grass snakes loose in the nuns' quarters.

By the time we could get back to our food cache, the bananas were turning brown. We ate them all anyway. Never again did I particularly like bananas.

The next time I remembered to calculate the time until Paradise Regained on my calendar pad, the number had dropped to sixty-five. And during those tense days I had not once thought of that damned Martin Luther. Come to think about it, I hadn't even thought about sex either.

CHAPTER 2 / *Lost*

Against all logical and theological odds, I graduated from Mount Saint Francis and proceeded onward to the Novitiate year, and then to acceptance into the Franciscan Order, taking temporary trial vows of obedience, chastity, and poverty, and moving then to a seminary college in Michigan and another in Ohio. I wanted more than ever to go home, but the mental fear of disobeying God's will kept me in thrall. The recognition that I received occasionally made thralldom endurable. Among the devout homefolks I was thought of now as a "man of God," an agonizing mental torture for me since I knew I was a heretic whose dreams seeped with gross sexual fantasies. But a more powerful conceit that kept me from going back to the land I yearned for was the flattering encouragement given to me by my teachers. They continued to praise what they called my original thinking and what they considered my talent for writing—all because I scored high on an IQ test. I was told that I was marked for much higher education than Franciscans usually pursued—*if* the rough edges of my character could be smoothed.

All this only increased my mental agony because I knew how stupid I could be sometimes (metaphysics and mechanics both puzzled me) and because I did not think that these earnest professors understood the first thing about good writing and so were poor judges of my clumsy efforts. I kept thinking that if I were as smart as they kept saying I was, why wouldn't anyone listen to what I had to say?

"I don't think I can stand wearing these long, black robes any longer," I said to Bee and Clutch one hot July night as we sat hunched around the radio in the recreation room at the Novitiate in Angola, Indiana. The Novitiate year was supposed to shape us into models of unquestioning obedience to our superiors. "Too damn hot."

"Not so bad if you don't wear anything under them," Clutch said.

"Oh, sure. Ole Hube would have a stroke if we did that," Bee said. Father Hubert was our novice master—our master sergeant, so to speak.

"Not if he didn't find out."

"But wouldn't it make more sense if our uniform were jeans and T-shirts?" I said. "These robes just put people off. And you can't do any real work while wearing them."

Bee laughed. "You're not going to have to do any real work. They're going to make a big time professor out of you."

"You'll spend your days defending concepts like why there are three divine persons in one God," Clutch said, grinning. "You won't ever have to worry about providing yourself with food, clothing and shelter."

"You know something?" I replied. "I don't see what difference it would make if there were thirty-three divine persons in one God or none. Does anyone really give a shit? I don't like all this doctrinal stuff, all this sanctimony and ceremony, all this trivial pursuit of hierarchy. I want to be like an Amish minister. Work right along with my people. You sure as hell can't wear one of these robes out making hay."

"On second thought, maybe they won't make a big shot professor out of you," Bee said. "You'll be lucky to get ordained at all."

I almost said I didn't care, but held my tongue. I was dangerously close to revealing my heresy, which I didn't even want my closest friends to know about. Fortunately, the bell rang, summoning us to chapel, where we spent several hours a day. This particular session was for a half hour of meditation before going into our daily round of chanting Latin prayers none of us could translate.

To endure "meditation" I usually riffled through my file of home memories and selected one to concentrate on, somewhat like putting a record on the phonograph player. I liked to play a memory game. I would mark off in my mind a certain stretch of the creek that ran through the home farm, and then walk mentally along it, trying to remember an event connected with every step of the way. Starting with the cliff-swallow nest holes in the creek bank, for instance, next came the big rock with the fossils in it; next the place where Marilyn found an arrowhead; next the fording place where the old sow couldn't get off the ice; next the big oak tree, shading our swimming hole; next the place where we had burned the big log for the neighborhood Fourth of July party; next the elm tree where Dad and the hired man made a rope swing out over the water; next the place where a raccoon had dragged our dog Brownie into the water and almost drowned him.

The hardest memory game was trying to remember every hickory tree in Kerr's woods that produced good, easily cracked nuts. We had names for some of the those trees and that helped.

But today I decided to replay the hockey game where our tribe of kinfolks beat the town pups when I was in the seventh grade. The altar in front of me disappeared, and in its place rose a vision of a crackling campfire on the banks of Grandpaw Rall's frozen pond.

"I've got a plan," Bernard said mysteriously. Being the oldest of the neighborhood cousins, he was our leader, especially in critical times like this. We had just been beaten in hockey by a bunch of boys from *town*. They had whipped us by the simple gambit of breaking our homemade sticks, made from tree branches, with their stronger store-bought ones and scoring goals while we were shorthanded because one player or another was up in the woods trying to find an appropriately bent new branch. And when the town pups left, one of them said that we should stick to clod-hopping and stay off ice skates.

It was one thing to be ridiculed because we were Catholics. In the realm of religion we could almost understand the philosophy of turning the other cheek, especially since we believed our detractors were all going to hell anyway. But to suffer insults because we were farmers was something else entirely. We might render to God the things that were God's, but we would render to Caesar exactly what Caesar deserved.

"I'm going to put together some hockey sticks out of white oak that'll make toothpicks out of theirs," Bernard said solemnly. "And I'm going to make sure Uncle Jerry and Uncle Lawrence and Uncle Pete are all there to play when the town pups come tomorrow."

"Yeah," said Egger. "If Uncle Pete plays, he'll use 'Old Hickory.'" Uncle Pete had carved Old Hickory out of a second-growth hickory sapling with an angled root stub at the end. It was not much good for scooting the puck along, but it was hell on shins.

"And Uncle Lawrence will wear his long racer skates that make him the fastest thing on ice," Bernard said.

"And Uncle Jerry—I mean my Dad—will wring their necks if they call us clodhoppers," I said.

By noon the next day, we had girded for battle. Since it was Sunday, it was not difficult to talk Dad into playing. Actually, he and Uncle Lawrence and Uncle Pete almost always played no matter what the day. The ice was not often fit for skating. So when it was, they generally dropped whatever they were doing, which at this time of year was hauling manure, and hauled us kids to the pond instead. We did not have to wait for weekends, like poor city people did.

Soon a couple of cars full of town pups rolled up with a few even older and bigger players than the day before. "The bigger they are, the harder they'll thall," Eddie said. He had trouble with his f's, but for only a fifth-grader, he could skate rings around most of us. Bernard gave him one of his special white-oak sticks. Egger and Donny and Paul, the next best skaters, got one too.

Our brand of hockey had very few rules to it. There was no limit to the number of players. A pair of boots set about three feet apart at each end of the pond served as goals. Play ended with injury or exhaustion, whichever came first.

The town pups acted friendly, but we spoke few words to them. Yesterday had been for fun till the matter of clodhoppers had been raised; today we meant to have war. Everyone just skated around tensely until Uncle Lawrence grabbed the puck and proceeded to the center of the pond.

"Let's get going," he yelled. The blades of his racer skates were at least eighteen inches long, and looked longer. The town pups stared at them with bulging eyes.

Bernard, our best player, squared off with the biggest of the town pups, a fellow everyone called Fishbait, except Eddie, who pronounced it Thishbait. Uncle Lawrence held the puck above their crossed hockey sticks, where the thick white-oak handle was connected to the angled piece of hickory at the business end of the stick.

"Hockey one, hockey two, hockey three," he chanted, then dropped the puck between the two players.

"Thwack!" The two sticks smacked each other as the puck bounced away and Fishbait's stick splintered at the neck.

"Goddam," he muttered and headed for his car to get a replacement. Bernard smiled angelically. Uncle Lawrence stole the puck out of the knot of stunned players and quick as a flash hurtled down the ice, rocketing the puck between the boots while he roared in glee.

After that, the town pups got organized and the game proceeded in the insane way our games were played. Up and down the ice the knot of players moved, like a little tornado, a broken stick or a blasphemy occasionally flying out of the maelstrom. Periodically a human form emerged from the melee and crawled to the shoreline bonfire to nurture fresh wounds. Finally the puck squirted loose from the pack and slid toward our goal. This was the moment all the sadists playing the game dearly loved, especially Dad, Uncle Lawrence, and Fishbait. As the puck bore down on the goal, the offensive players bore down on the puck, the defensive players bore down on the offensive players, and Donny, our goalie, bore down on the ice as he watched his life drawing to a close. The human wave broke over him. Sticks split, steel sparked, teeth chipped, flesh rent. Everything passed through the goal except the puck, which was already on its way toward the other end of the pond, having been passed up in the mad dash. Too poor a skater to keep up with the crowd, I now found myself feebly guiding it the other way until the mob overtook me and repeated the same onslaught on the town pups' goal. Dad had more speed than his body could keep up with. He was out ahead of the crowd, but as Fishbait closed in on him, he lost his balance, his feet flew almost as high in the air as his stick, and the rest of the gang roared past him on the way to the goal. Again the human wave broke over the town pups' goalie and again the puck hopped away without a score, as if it had a mind of its own. Now Fishbait had the puck with open ice ahead. He churned toward our goal all alone, with Uncle Lawrence gaining on him. Donny, guarding the goal, resigned himself to God and laid down in front of the boots to block the shot with his body. But as Fishbait roared toward him, his eye on Uncle Lawrence coming up from the rear, a small figure shot out from the shoreline, stole the puck away, and slammed it into the cattails at the edge of the pond. It was Marilyn, who was not supposed to play with the big kids.

"Way to go, way to go!" we cheered her, especially Dad.

"Mom will have a conniption if she finds out you played against the town pups," I added.

"Why should boys have all the fun?" she retorted.

But the brilliance of her defensive move was only now becoming apparent. Three town pups skated into the cattails to fetch the puck. They should have wondered why none of the farm kids followed them. One after the other, the three sank through the weak ice around the cattails.

"Goddam," each of them said in turn.

"Hooooeee!" I yelled. "Don't see any clodhoppers dumb enough to do that, do you?"

Back and forth the ebb and flow of hockey players slid and tumbled. For half an hour, the puck refused to go through either goal. Then Fishbait and a teammate he called Heinie railroaded Bernard off into the cattails and ricocheted the puck off Donny's leg for a goal. Donny rolled on the ice in agony. Uncle Pete believed he would guard goal awhile.

Again Fishbait and Heinie broke loose from the pack with the puck and raced toward the goal. But instead of little Donny, there was stout old Uncle Pete standing in the way. Fishbait decided he'd just take the old man into the goal with the puck. As he lowered his head to ram Uncle Pete, Old Hickory rose into the air like a golf club and whistled forward in a flashing blur.

"Thwack!" Fishbait's stick flew off in two pieces and Fishbait himself bounced off Uncle Pete as from a concrete wall.

Eddie flitted into the scene like a fly, grabbed the puck with his stick and headed the other way. "That'll teach ya, Thishbait! That'll teach ya!" he yelled over his shoulder. At this point, the rest of the players, too weak from exhaustion and laughter to continue, sank to the ice as they watched little Eddie skate tauntingly for the other goal, just out of reach of an angry Fishbait, flailing an ineffective piece of broken stick. In a few seconds we were ahead 2 to 1, and that's the way the game ended.

"FRIAR BLAISE, STAND UP!" The present exploded upon me with a strident bark from Hube. Blaise was my religious name —sounded like a horse's name, Marilyn said—and I was supposed to be on my feet to begin chanting the breviary for the day. Oh God, I was going to catch hell again.

Catching hell was routine for me. One day in class, Hube was trying to teach us how we must "subsume our wills to the will of God," the theological point that was at the source of all my anguish. He used as an example the old monastic tradition that a Friar not only must plant cabbages upside down if ordered to do so, but must believe that planting cabbages upside down was indeed the correct thing to do.

"That's not possible," I blurted. "If your mind *knows* planting cabbages upside down is the wrong way, you can't make yourself believe it *is* the right way." My voice sounded thin, coming from afar, from some idiot I didn't know.

"There is a wisdom that transcends puny reason," Hube rumbled ominously. Short, solid, and square, especially around the jaw, he had the right physique for a linebacker, and I was sure he could kill me with one blow. "Perfect obedience rises above earthly considerations."

Bee was staring desperately at me, not believing I could be so stupid as to spout off this way. But I thought surely that I was expressing an undeniable fact. "All I'm saying," I continued, my voice quavering, "is that you can't force your mind to agree with what it can't agree with. You can pretend. Heaven knows, you can pretend."

Hube's eyelids came together, squaring off even his pupils. The lines of his mouth flattened out and his jaw jutted forward. Now his whole face looked to me like a checkerboard, all little squares making one big square pushing out toward me like the prow of a river scow. He appeared to hover on the edge of anger, his emotion contained only by force of all that binding, fleshy geometry.

"Well, you can, Friar, when you learn the true meaning of obedience. And. You. Will. Learn. That."

A few days later, I brushed against a picture of Pope Pius XII hanging on the wall of the hallway leading to chapel. I think Shorty shoved me but that was little comfort. The picture fell on the floor. I picked it up and noticed with dismay that the glass had cracked, the crack looking like a thunderbolt erupting out of the pope's mouth, giving him a lopsided grimace as if he had listened too long to Cardinal Tisserand objecting to his policies. I was tempted to laugh, although now I was in trouble. Breaking anything, much less a picture of a pope, meant being punished—like having to do the dishes alone for a week. Maybe I could just hang it up again before Hube arrived on the scene and he'd never notice.

I had just about positioned the picture back on its hanger when thunder rolled in behind me. "What are you doing?!" Hube roared.

Taken unawares, I jumped and so did the picture, my fingers chasing it desperately through the air as it crashed once more to the floor. Now there was another crack that seemed to go in one of the pope's ears and out the other, like most of Cardinal Tisserand's advice. Hube's lips began to quiver. His glasses slowly slid down his nose as they always did when he went into his act of awful outrage.

"Answer me!" he roared.

My tongue wouldn't move. No, my tongue was okay. I could feel it wobble vigorously against my teeth. It was my mouth that was paralyzed. I didn't think my heart was beating either. No one had ever spoken to me like this before.

"What are you trying to say?" he bawled into my face. I felt delirium approaching. I was back home in the barn, ten years old, swinging from one mow to the other on the hay rope. I landed short, slid off the edge of the mow and fell to the floor. I lay there, the wind knocked out of me, Mom kneeling over me, crying, asking me if I was all right. I knew I was okay, but I could not breathe, could not tell her not to cry. Not being able to talk, not being able to breathe, though my mind was perfectly clear in knowing that I must breathe, I wondered if this was like dying. Then, just as blackness surrounded me, I felt the first, short, blessed pumpings of my lungs.

"MY HEART ALMOST STOPPED BEATING!" I blurted insanely. Presence of mind swiftly returning, I clapped my hand to my mouth. Shorty giggled. Everyone started laughing.

Hube's demeanor changed. Up to now he had simply been in standard procedural mode: humiliate the poor bastard. Now he knew that he had a special problem to solve. Laughter separated men from beasts, a sure sign of the kind of bold rationality that had no place in these halls where it was his duty to inculcate blind obedience. Holding the cracked picture of the pope before him like a banner, he waded into battle for the Lord.

"Funny is it? By God I'll show you how funny it is!" He herded us into a classroom and commanded us to be seated.

"Now you laugh, young fellow," he growled at Shorty. "AND DON'T QUIT LAUGHING UNTIL I TELL YOU!"

Shorty tried to laugh. He cranked out noises like an old Fordson tractor; he ho-hoed like a degenerate Santa Claus.

"Everybody laugh!"

Everybody laughed.

"LOUDER!"

Everybody laughed louder.

"Friar Blaise, face the class and do a solo laugh."

I tried. I sounded like a leghorn rooster.

Hube shifted into another gear. "What's so funny?" He glared at me.

I sat down while I tried to think of what to say.

"Do I have to tell you to stand up when you're addressing a priest, Friar? Didn't they teach you anything at Mount Saint Francis? What is your name and STAND UP WHEN I TALK TO YOU!"

"Yes, Father." I stood up, terrified out of my mind. "My name is Gene Logsdon."

"Gene Logsdon is dead, Friar. Gene Logsdon doesn't exist. Now you repeat after me twenty times: 'My name is Friar'"—he paused as if he could not remember—"'whatever it is.'"

"My name is Friar Blaise. My name. . . ."

"That's not what I told you to repeat."

"My name is Friar Whatever It Is. My name is Friar Whatever It Is. My name. . . .

"Why don't you laugh now, Friar Howard? Don't you think it's funny that this nincompoop doesn't even know his own name?" He paused. "If I ever hear that barbaric yelp of yours in these halls again, you'll wish to God you'd have joined the army."

Then he stalked abruptly out, returned momentarily, and ordered me to come to his office after chapel.

I tried to prepare myself for another browbeating. Perhaps I should just pack up and skip town, as Bee suggested. To hit a priest, the only other alternative that appealed to me, meant instant excommunication. And linebacker Hube might break my skull in return. In fear and trepidation I entered his office. To my astonishment, he was a different man. Kindness washed off of him in great bubbling suds of chuckles and smiles. He was smoking, however, distracting to me since I craved nicotine but had nothing to smoke. He didn't inhale, but merely puffed and expelled great whorls of blue smoke as if to torment me. But if I sucked in strongly enough, I could get a mild hit. He mixed chitchat with the smoke as if we were old pals. Finally he got down to business as I waited to hear that I was expelled.

"Are you happy here?" he asked gently.

I didn't know what to answer. What was happy? Hube assured me that he was. How could anyone be happy browbeating other people around every day? That was his job, he protested. He didn't like it either. Well, there was old duty again. How was that happy? I thought I had him there. But he switched bats.

"What would you like to do once you're a priest?" he asked.

"Teach and write," I said. That was easy. I threw in teaching to make it sound more respectable.

"Couldn't one be a writer and a teacher without being a priest?" Hube suggested, again very gently.

He left the question hanging in the air with his blue smoke for possible further inhalation. I decided it was a good time to voice a theory I had about myself. I knew there were physical and mental problems that might bar a person from the priesthood. For awhile I thought I had found one that applied to me. Although I was almost totally ignorant of sexual matters beyond the basic act of copulation, learned early on from being around farm animals, I wondered, based on the wildly imaginative sexual dreams that I was experiencing, if maybe I might be some kind of pervert. I decided to suggest the possibility. By now he had tried to brutalize my spirit so often that I didn't care what he thought of me.

"Father Hubert, I think there's something wrong with me," I said, up through the delicious blue smoke.

"There's something wrong with all of us, Friar," he said, much more kindly than he had ever spoken to me before. "It's usually a good sign if you are aware of it. The ones I worry about are those who don't think there's anything wrong with them."

I took a deep breath. I had to get it out all at once or my voice might fail me. "I have grossly erotic dreams at night that almost always end in nocturnal emissions. Orgasms." (I had looked the word up but wasn't sure that I was using it correctly. At least it sounded dreadful.)

Hube did not so much as flicker an eye. "That's normal, my son," he said. "You might be a little more highly sexed than the norm but nothing to feel guilty about." After a pause, he grew stern again. "Which means you must be extraordinarily disciplined."

So the system foiled me again.

Miraculously, our whole class graduated out of the Novitiate, losing only one member, Carl, which greatly upset me because he was our best baseball player. Without him, our reputation of being able to beat every other class in the seminary was endangered. We proceeded then to the seminary college along the Grand River in Michigan, a former millionaire's mansion that the order named Cupertino College. Bee and I walked in awe past the swimming pool, formal gardens, and through the sprawling house with its gold brocade wallpaper. "If this happens when you take the vow of poverty, what lies in store for us from the vow of chastity?" he remarked with a faint smile.

Our new Rector, Benedict, arrived in a few months, a sallow little man of about sixty who gradually revealed what we decided, on the strength of one course in abnormal psychology, serious neurotic tendencies. After the book *The Caine Mutiny* came out, I always referred to him as Father Queeg. In a good mood, he would joke and banter with us. On bad days, he would explode at the most minor provocation. He was haunted by suspicion that we were committing major transgressions of the rules that he couldn't catch us at. He became convinced that the teenage girls from the farm next to us were at night using our swimming pool, which was located a considerable distance from the mansion, and that we had either already joined them or were about to. A notice went up on the bulletin board, threatening everything except excommunication for anyone going to the pool after dark.

Hopefully, we started going to the pool after dark. No girls.

I was not disappointed because I was having my own hallucinations. Father John, who held high office in our Franciscan Province and at the new Bellarmine College in Louisville, and a man I always liked, said he wanted me to pursue a doctorate in English so I could teach and write at Bellarmine. After that, my head high in the airy atmosphere of recognition, I decided that I was destined to become a famous novelist. The fact that there were no girls in the pool, but only in Father Queeg's mind, would make a better story than if girls really were swimming there. Father Queeg was going to be my ticket to fame and fortune. All I had to do was observe and write down what happened.

I began to write a novel about seminary life. I wrote during class, during chapel, in bed, and while boating on the river. Sometimes I actually wrote something on paper. I took to walking at night, as sure as a madman that I was destined for great literary pursuits. I told Bee about my eerie feeling.

"Don't start worrying about it until you hear voices of beautiful girls swimming in the pool," he answered.

When I did write something on paper, the story quickly turned into a fantasy about a young farmer who had a whole lot more sense than ever to leave home grounds. For two years I poured on paper an idealized version of the life on the home farm, escaping by that means, the anguish of my real life. The more I wrote, the more I edged toward risking God's wrath and becoming my fantasy farmer in real life. But just when I thought I could not stand Queeg one day more, the Franciscans bought a new seminary property located on a farm in a far-off, romantic-sounding place called Minnesota. Queeg would be left behind. Maybe I'd stay on one more year, just to see what life in such a faraway place was like. Now that I was almost sure I would never become a priest, masquerading as a seminarian didn't seem so reprehensible.

CHAPTER 3 / *Realizing the Truth*

I climbed up to the top of the high pasture knoll on the farm that the seminary had rented and tried to make some sense out of my cockeyed life. All hell had broken loose. The knoll, overlooking little Wasserman Lake was my favorite retreat when the insanities of my twenty-four years pressed too hard upon me. I gazed out over miles of peaceful Minnesota dairyland, dotted with farmsteads, green alfalfa fields, yellow oat fields, and little blue lakes, beautiful to a farmer's eyes beyond any telling of it. All this countryside lay in sweet, rural serenity, awaiting, like a naive country virgin, violation by the urban out-migration that was starting to come from the Twin Cities. The village of Chanhassen, a few miles beyond visibility from the knoll, was typical: so small that Main Street was the only street, with farm fields pushing up behind the stores and homes that lined it. Two bars and a diner bulked up the "downtown" along with several retail shops and a grocery, plus the necessary ball diamond at one edge of town and a church at the other.

I loved to sit disguised in jeans and cowboy hat in any of the bars or diners of the nearby rural villages and watch the daily drama of life unfold. Seminary rules forbade entering such places without permission, of course, but that added to the adventure. I never had money, but Jim, the Franciscan lay brother whom I worked with on the farm and my close friend, carried cash for farm business purposes, and he would treat me to a cup of coffee or mug of beer. We had to have some excuse to sit there watching and listening to the theater of the real world.

(A rough, bewhiskered man saunters slowly in, sits down on a bar stool, staring at the waitress all the while. Without a trace of anger he says: "Goddamn you, Mabel. You gave me the clap, you know.")

(A group of glum and silent farmers drink coffee around a diner table and contemplate the specter of surplus crops driving down farm prices below the cost of production. One of them finally says: "If we have another good year like this one, we'll all be ruined.")

(In the Stagecoach Inn, where horses hunch at the hitch rail outside, the waiters wear pistols on their belts as part of the decor, but one of them really does draw his gun and shoot someone over a lover's quarrel. I was sorely disappointed that I was not there when it happened.)

(From the windows of the Shakopee Inn, still thriving on the high banks above the Minnesota River, customers in the last century once watched a real Indian battle on the plain across the river. What modern Theater of the Living Arts could top that?)

Sitting atop the pasture knoll, I took stock of the last three years. Life had become almost wonderful for me since coming to Minnesota, which explained why I had not yet gotten up the courage to "endanger my immortal soul" by quitting the seminary, even though by now I knew that I must. My new-found contentment was why all hell was suddenly breaking loose in my life. At Jim's and my urging, our superiors had rented a farm to go along with the few acres that had come with the seminary so that, as we argued, we could produce all of the seminary's basic food. Whether or not that was a smart move was debatable, but for me it was almost Paradise Now. Dispensed from the routine of a normal seminary schedule so that I could help Jim on the farm until more lay brothers were recruited, I took more than full advantage of the situation and lived the life of a farmer more than of a seminarian.

I was up early in the morning to milk the cows and clean the barn, avoiding most of the chapel hours the other friars attended, and then, after philosophy and theology classes in the forenoon, which I also sometimes was able to wangle my way out of, off to the barn and fields as quickly as I could, working far enough into the evening hours to avoid the rest of the liturgical and prayer-filled routine that I disliked. It struck me that maybe God had in mind for me to become a lay brother like Jim, which was what Bee had done. In the meantime, I was leading a fairy tale existence somewhere in the no-man's-land between conventional monastic life and conventional American life, a cross between Friar Tuck and an Amish dairyman. Why go home just now, when I was almost home right here?

But almost home was a far place from home. As I sat on the knoll, I watched a farm family at work in a cornfield next to our rented land and knew that for sure. The farmer and his wife and children were moving with horses and wagon across a field of corn shocks, picking up ears that the binder had knocked on the ground, just like our family had done what seemed now like centuries ago. Then, in absolute *déjà vu*, I watched the father beckon his children around him, skin back the husk from an ear he had picked up, and hurl the ear high into the air, like Dad had done. The children shouted with glee as the ear, guided by its husk-tail, soared in a high arc and came back to earth tip first. We had called them corn rockets. I was filled with a terrible desire to be that man, to be in my cornfield with *my* family, hurling corn rockets in the air.

My mind wrenched me back to my current misery, the source of which was not my secret heresy, or quandaries about the will of God, or even longing for home, at least not directly. The guardian in charge of us, whom we called Doc, had seemed to me a wonderfully sane and fair man, but last night he had taken an electric carpenter's saw and tried to cut our boat in half. My comrades and I, known within the seminary as the Sonuvabitchin' Davy Crockett boys, a name we flaunted, had been weeks working on the boat, in which we planned to cruise up and down the nearby Minnesota River.

"Goddam. God*dam*," Clutch said when he had delivered the news to me. "Doc did it. He admitted it. I'm gonna saw his goddam desk in half."

Donny, whose doughty attitude always amazed me, took a different approach. "The saw cut a pretty jagged hole in the bottom of the boat, but it can be patched," he said. "Wonder Doc didn't cut his arm off with the blade in backwards like that."

I was too stunned to know what to say. What kind of a snake pit was I living in, to provoke a priest who normally governed by love and persuasion to do such a thing? Sitting in my room, trying to make sense of it, I noticed Doc standing at the door, glowering in his black robes like a panther.

"Why, oh, why?" I asked.

"I've tried every kind way I could think of to convince you and your friends that you were using all your energies and abilities for worldly matters instead of devoting yourselves to spiritual values. You spend all your time following your will, not God's will."

So there it was again. God's will. Doc liked me, I knew. He was like a real father who wanted me to follow in his footsteps so badly that he would try almost anything to make it happen, driven not by meanness but out of his unquestioning faith in his idea of God. But I'd had enough.

"Oh, so you know what God's will is, do you?" I blazed. "Who the hell says you're that smart? Who imparted infallibility on you? By what total arrogance do you assume you know the will of God? Maybe God told me to build that boat. How the hell do you know? If God wanted you to wreck our boat, how come He let you put the blade in backwards?"

Doc had had enough too. He grabbed my guitar—the only thing in the room I cared about, and he knew it—smashed it over the corner of my desk, threw the pieces on the floor, and stalked out.

I was too stunned at this totally foreign kind of behavior to even become enraged. I just sat there, a totality of blackness blotting out any thinking at all. Finally I walked outside, climbed in the farm truck, and, asking permission of no one, drove to the

farm, some ten miles from the seminary. I walked up the hill where
I now sat, nursing a terrible rage.

Doc was right. I was following my own will, escaping my
proper life as a seminarian much more than the work of the farm
required. But was that really wrong? I had so far passed all the
school courses required of me. Beyond that, I was working my ass
off doing what the "holier" friars would not or could not do. Doc
himself said farm work could be a form of prayer. I wasn't involved
in any serious transgressions of the rules, nor were my friends—
not in any homosexual relationships, not chasing women, not getting drunk. Why should we be singled out as the bad boys of the
community?

Something in a field below me, in the opposite direction of
the family picking up corn, caught my eye and interrupted my
dark thoughts. A girl on horseback herding cows had appeared
over the brow of a lower hill. If only I were an artist, what a picture that would make! I recognized her, having a nodding acquain-
tance with most of the neighbors from helping with the oats
threshing on all the nearby farms. I watched her for awhile, unaware that she had spotted me too. She waved. I waved back. She
wheeled her horse and galloped to the fenceline between us. I could
hardly not go down to talk to her. But why was I running?

At the fence, we exchanged smiles. When we had threshed
oats at her family's farm last year, she had remained aloof, distant,
bringing the customary mid-morning and mid-afternoon lunches
to the field and serving dinner at the house without comment,
always appearing out of nowhere when her aging father called for
her. I'd never really paid much attention to her, but now I noticed
her striking, high cheekbones, supple body in the saddle, the way
her leg curved alluringly down the side of the horse, and her rich
auburn hair ruffling in the wind.

"Are you worried about the cows bloating on that alfalfa?" I
asked, at a loss for something to say.

"They're used to it," she said. "Won't hurt them. It's a hungry
cow on frosted alfalfa you have to worry about."

Hmmm. In my world, girls didn't have that kind of knowledge at their fingertips, not even my sister Marilyn, who was the smartest person I knew. "Do you get tired herding the cows out here all alone?"

"Oh, no. This is my favorite job," she said. "I like to be alone. It's so peaceful out here. Is that why you're up on the knoll?"

"Well, yes," I said. "I love to look out over the farms. You can see for miles from up there."

"I go up there a lot myself," she said, nodding in agreement. "How do you think that knoll got there like that? Looks like a big wart. It's different from the other hills."

"Where I come from in Ohio, people would suspect it was an Indian mound," I said. "But I suppose a glacier formed it." Then I added playfully, to see how she would react: "Maybe it's magic."

She studied me. She didn't seem to put much stock in romantic notions like that. We talked on about horses and cows and other little everyday, humdrum activities of farm life. What a blessed relief from the browbeating plunges into the black pits of speculation about the will of God. I found myself discussing some of my secret things: how the honking Canada geese sounded so happy going north in the spring and so forlorn going south in the fall, although the sound itself was exactly the same. She told me about the fawn she had caught after its mother had been killed by a hunter, and how she raised it on a baby bottle. I hadn't thought any woman cared about wildlife and farming ways like I did. Suddenly she cocked her eye at the sun. "Heavens, it's past time to get the cows home for milking."

As I drove back to the seminary, I was aware that my spirit had lifted. I was spinning out of orbit into space I had never journeyed before. I spoke to no one and no one spoke to me. Didn't matter. Somehow, for the first time, I felt like my own man. The news of the broken guitar had spread through the seminary and everyone except my closest friends acted as if I had leprosy. So what. Being a loner suddenly agreed with me. Doc didn't ask where I had been and I volunteered nothing.

The next day I could no more stop myself from going over to the farm than I could stop eating. Again I drove away, daring anyone to try to stop me.

She brought another horse along this time. "Just in case," she said, and we laughed, knowing each other's mind. As I climbed into the saddle, she cried, "Race you!" and we tore over the pasture at full gallop, the wind blowing my mind clean and sweet of the musty dregs of duty-driven religion. I noted, with keen pleasure, that she kept right up, and that she was laughing as delightedly as I was. Reining in, we studied each other silently. Smiles. "Do you care if I call you 'Yellow Rose'?" I asked. That was my favorite song at the moment.

She looked at me and laughed, not knowing what to make of me. After that, I found all kinds of excuses to go to the farm in hopes of seeing her.

"What are you going to do when you grow up," I asked her once with a playful air, for she was hardly five years younger than I.

"I don't know," she sighed. "My parents say I should get a job in town, but I want to farm with Dad. Girls aren't supposed to want to farm."

"Yeah, I know the feeling."

"I think eventually I'll go to Alaska and homestead," she said. "I want to get away from cities and crowds."

"I want to get a little ranch in a valley where the sun comes up at one end and goes down on the other end and no one can get in unless I say so," I said.

She looked surprised. "But priests don't do that, do they?"

"I'm not going to be a priest," I said. It was the first time I had uttered those words to another person.

Alone, I wondered if I were falling in love or if I were just profoundly angry at everything in my seminary life. I asked an old priest whom I thought was worldly-wise how a person could tell if he were in love. He immediately assumed I was having some kind of sexual affair.

"Oh, for God's sake," I said and stormed out of the room. I supposed I only confirmed his suspicions. Was sex the *only* thing humans thought about?

I tried to pray, but it was like counting bricks on a very large house. Why could I not gaze hypnotically at the altar and draw some secret solace from on high as other friars seemed to do? In public I could babble prayers, but in private, talking to God was an embarrassing pretension. What could I say to Someone who knew everything?

Donny patched up the boat, good as new, and Doc said nothing more about it, evidently thinking he had made his point. But nothing could patch the rift between the seminary and me. Even the feeling of friendship and loyalty I had felt for my comrades was passing. It was all over. But later that month threshing began, the highlight of the year for me, and as in the past Jim and I and Denny and Donny and Zeke would follow the thresher from farm to farm, representing the seminary in the threshing ring. I waited for Doc to relieve me of that work because he knew I loved it. But maybe he did not want to bring the crisis to a head. Maybe he divined that if he tried that, I'd do it anyway, to hell with the vow of obedience. I had moved beyond the fear of any witch-doctor hierarchy.

Communal threshing, which back home had passed from history in the late thirties, and remained only a dim memory to me, was still in vogue in this part of Minnesota in the early fifties. A neighborhood of farmers, jointly owning a threshing machine, moved from farm to farm to harvest the oat crop. By such mutual interest, farmers had for centuries developed a cooperative spirit that transcended individual friendships and enmities alike and so made the only kind of community that was genuine—one with a mutual, shared economy. We seminarians warmed to this mutuality, being ourselves the heirs of an ancient but similar monastic economy.

For me, with feet in both agrarian and religious traditional communities, with the perspective of having known the threshing ring as a child, as if in another life, and now with Yellow Rose in the background, the communal harvest became almost a mystical experience. I was stepping back into the past, to horse-farming days that I kept much holier in my mind than I suppose they really were, and I was transported. Standing on top of the thresher, wheeling the blower into position over the mounting straw stack, knowing that Yellow Rose was watching, I felt like I was God, or, remembering Uncle Ade atop the haystack with his red bandanna cowboy-like over his face, at least Tom Mix. I knew that fate was granting me the sad privilege of living the last days of a Christian rural tradition that had fostered not just the family farm, but the self-subsistent monastery too. They existed side by side, and the circumstances that brought one down would bring down the other. Farmers were going to the factories and friars to the universities. Not only were these days the last occasions of community threshing with horses outside the Amish enclaves, but the last years of subsistent monastery life too. *The brick building we worked so hard to restore into our seminary would, within thirty years, be abandoned and crumble to the ground right in step with the decline of traditional family farming.*

But for the moment, I rode very tall in the saddle. Zany banter along with oat chaff filled the air. Jim, approaching the thresher on a wagon load of oat bundles, crowed like a rooster: "I'm the best in the West!" He had been a bartender before he became a Franciscan.

"Don't you mean 'beast from the East'?" Denny roared up at him above the hum and throb of the machine.

"I think he means 'mouth from the South,'" Donny chimed in, even louder.

Jim, echoing a line from the fast-draw westerns we loved, shouted back: "Fill your hand, you sonuvabitch."

An older farmer in the threshing ring by the name of Krause listened slack-jawed to our constant droll chatter. He had been told that we were monks, and he had no idea monks would talk and act like we did. But finally he seemed to approve and quickly carved a niche for himself in our conversation. "I want to warn you that Minnesota gumbo is the stickiest substance in the world," he said one day when we were discussing soils. "You hafta walk fast on it after a rain or you'll get stuck. Plumb hung up." He paused to see what effect that information might have on us and then continued in woebegone Norwegian twang: "If you get that stuff on your boot, you gotta kick five times to get it off. Five times. Four won't do it and six is one too many."

Donny and I started laughing. Krause looked offended, which made his lower lip stick out more than the snuff under it would warrant. "You don't believe it, by God, you just try it. You see, you gotta conserve your energy in farming. If you don't use your head, you have to use your hands and feet, and that'll eventually kill you."

Loading oat shocks on a wagon out in the field, I watched Yellow Rose come riding from the house with a big basket of sandwiches.

"There is something particularly beautiful about a girl on a horse," Zeke rumbled, leaning on his fork. "Especially when she is bringing food."

We both laughed. Previously I would have answered his remark with one equally as witty, but now I could not trust myself to say anything about Yellow Rose. When she handed me a sandwich, we exchanged piercing glances, but then I could only stare at the ground and mumble my thanks. It occurred to me that if I were really in love, and since I was leaving the seminary anyway, I would have talked openly to her and not given a damn what anyone thought.

Fortunately, Krause was there to occupy our attention. He jabbed his fork into one of the tied bundles that made up the shock and lifted it over his head to serve as a sun shade. "Hell yes, it makes you cooler," he countered in response to our quizzical grins. Watching us throw the bundles onto a wagon, he shook his head. "If you just throw 'em on every whichaway like that, you can't get much of a load on. You gotta rack 'em up around the outside like cordwood with the butts all facing out. Otherwise they might all fall off going around these goddam steep hills. If these fields were laid out right, you could roll them round hay bales by gravity right to the barn. Be hell if you missed though. They'd roll right off the edge of the farm."

Krause destroyed my last dwindling respect for scholarly intellectualism. He asked me one day what I really thought about God. When I shrugged, not knowing exactly what to say to the wily old farmer, he answered his own question: "I don't believe in a hereafter, but I keep going to church just in case I'm wrong." I almost couldn't laugh. I knew that he had never been near a book of philosophy, if any book at all, and yet he was articulating succinctly the philosophically famous Pascalian Wager. Here was a man capable of matching wits with certified philosophers who would starve to death in his shoes. Who really was the more "educated"?

After harvest, I had little opportunity to see Yellow Rose, but I did manage to tell her that I was going home but hoped to come back sometime to see her. She had provided me with a great gift— a lovely, innocent, feminine look at the world far removed from the grim, pietistic, apodictic religiosity of monastic life. Unwittingly she probably saved me from a nervous breakdown. Thinking of the world she opened to me, I knew that by leaving the seminary, I could only save my soul, my Self, not lose it. I waited only for a tactful moment to announce my departure, accept the pitying judgment I would receive for "endangering my soul," and go through the procedure of being dispensed from vows.

One day, I was trying to carry a heavy fence post across a field when one of my professors approached. I liked him because his view of religion was more liberal and open-minded than most of the others. He helped with the post without asking or being asked, which was so unusual I knew something must be afoot.

"Why do you insist on doing work like this with a mind like yours?" he asked as we paused to rest our load. I could tell that he was sincere so I didn't try to disagree. He could not believe that a seemingly intelligent man might prefer farming to the classroom. Like everyone else I had discussed the point with, he evidently saw no possibility in combining the two. "We need scholars, not fencebuilders," he remarked. "I think you just do farm work as an escape." I still didn't answer, not only for lack of breath from carrying the heavy post, but because he might be right about that. But he was wrong about my being so intelligent. I could not get good grades in philosophy courses. I could not grasp metaphysics—though I was convinced metaphysicians were the biggest fakes since alchemists.

"Are you interested in studying in Rome?" he asked abruptly.

Oh, God. The rumor had been going around for awhile. Some of us were destined for universities in Rome, in Quebec, in Washington, in Saint Louis. Seminary colleges were to be closed. Too much intellectual inbreeding. I agreed with that, but oh, God, why me? Why did I want to work at farming, where I was sometimes inept with machinery, when I could go to some damn university and excel? Was I just being contrary? How could I tell this well-meaning professor that studying holy soil required more brilliance than studying Holy Scripture? I had no desire to go to Rome anyway, even as a tourist. Rome to me was a place of decadence and poor maintenance, living off the so-called glory of its past. Rome raped its own agriculture and that of all northern Africa to keep its aristocracy opulent enough to support artists painting fat angels on church ceilings.

There was no way I could articulate such radical agrarianism to this earnest young priest. I could only say no, I won't go, and then be honorable enough to leave the seminary immediately. I had had my three years of Brigadoon. It was time to get back to real earth.

But one more amazingly Brigadoonish incident took place that would forever convince me, no matter how much of a rationalist and humanist I considered myself, that there was such a thing as magic. Not long before I left for home, I was paying final homage to the magical farm where rural life and a lovely young woman had convinced me that God's will was whatever a person wanted it to be. I was getting a drink of water at the farmhouse pump. A teenage girl came up from the lake while I was drinking, towing a younger child in hand. The teenager smiled at me out of the most bewitching eyes I had ever seen. "Can we get a drink of water, please?" she asked in a rich southern drawl that sounded starkly foreign in this land of German gutterals, plaintive Scandinavian twangs, and clipped syllables of Twin City suburbanites. There was no aloofness, no fear, no even slight hesitancy in her manner, as might have been natural for a girl in a strange place, confronting a strange young man sweaty and dirty from work. Otherwise it was not too unusual for an occasional lake visitor to come to the house. I smiled back. For some reason her open and carefree manner amused me more than the incident seemed to justify. I walked over to the pump and drew a cup of water for her. I watched her intently as she drank. She returned my gaze just as intently and seemed in no hurry to empty the cup.

"Who *was* that?" I asked Zeke after she went back to the lake.

"Donny's kid sister. His family is visiting from Kentucky."

"What's her name?"

"Carol, I think."

Donny's kid sister. Carol. What eyes. I went back to work, but she remained lodged in some recess of my mind. Later that would make sense. I had just met the girl whom I would marry five years hence and live happily with ever after.

CHAPTER 4 / *The Log Cabin in the Woods*

Back home, circumstances plunged me into an even deeper melancholy than I had felt as a seminarian. Trying to become acclimated to the "real" world after ten years of monkish living, I was an awkward, ignorant traveler stumbling around in a foreign land. I was about ready to agree that Tom Wolfe was right about not being able to go home again, but for different reasons than those he gave. *I* could not "go home again" yet because I was too poor. My father could not afford to hire me full-time on the home place, and I was too broke to buy a candy bar, much less a piece of my own land. I had overcome the agony of believing that I could not go home because of "God's will" only to be stopped by a more formidable vexation: "economic will."

As I waited in frustration to be inducted into the army (to volunteer meant three years instead of two), I was so desperate in my desire to have my own place, to know home, that I started gathering rocks and piling them back on the hill next to Kerr's Woods, where Dad said I could build a house someday. I had a notion I could build cheaply with found stones and lumber. This mad idea turned out to be another stroke of magic because in lifting the huge rocks, I injured a disc in my spine. The army in 1957 wanted no part of a twenty-five-year-old inductee with back problems. Before I could be called back again, I passed my twenty-sixth birthday and did not have to go at all.

To my amazement, no one thought this was tremendously for-
tuitous except Marilyn. All the aunts and uncles and parents and
grandparents who had deemed it proper for me to go the seminary now opined that the army would have allowed me some time
to "mature" into the real world. "But I've been in the army for ten
years," I protested. Blank stares. My mind silently screamed in
frustration. What did these people who thought they were experts
on "the real world" really know? They were all full of myths too.

Even Yellow Rose, whom I telephoned, seemed diffident about
my escape from the draft. In an agony of loneliness and depression, I decided to go to Mount Saint Francis and see my friends,
Bee and Jim, who were now stationed there. We laughed and
played guitars through most of the night, remembering with sweet
sadness, like old army buddies, the rollicking days in Minnesota.
Next day Bee wanted to go out to visit Donny's family, the Downses, whom he had gotten to know well through Donny, at their
farm outside Louisville. I remembered Carol, but did not say so.

When we pulled into the driveway, there seemed to be Downses everywhere. Two or three brothers and father Downs tumbled
out of various barns and sheds, shouting greetings and pumping
our hands as if we were long lost friends. Two or three sisters and
mother Downs, also wreathed in smiles, appeared from garden
and kitchen. Were it not for the sparkling eyes, I would not have
recognized Carol, who had grown considerably. Her open manner, utterly without pretense, which characterized all the Downses,
again delighted me more than the situation warranted, but since
she was much younger than I, I pretended to take more notice of
her brother Jimmy's new blue convertible than of her.

"*My* car," Carol said, teasingly, eyeing her brother. "When
Jimmy goes to the air force, it's *my* car, my Bluebird."

Up somewhere in the leafy maple tree I was standing under, I
heard my voice descending with a most preposterous statement:
"Well, Jimmy, if you decide to sell it, I'd be interested."

"I don't know," he laughed. "You might have to take Carol as
part of the bargain."

I stole a sharp glance at her. Nothing registered there beyond the joke of it, but when I looked back at Jimmy, I swear there was just a certain pixie gleam in his eye. Or was I seeing a reflexion of my own eye?

I went back home revived in spirit beyond any reason I could put into words. The dismal feelings of the last two years had been swept away by Bee's humor and the Downses' innate gaiety. Dad and I started in on the corn harvest the next day and there was between us a settled feeling about what we were doing. I got a job running a ditching machine. It paid over a hundred dollars a week, more money than I thought I'd ever be able to make.

Then we decided to "get big or get out," as farmers were saying, and doubled the dairy herd. When that was still not enough to make a decent income, Dad expanded again and I quit running the ditcher to work full-time with him and my brother. Although three of us worked ourselves to both physical and nervous exhaustion, we could barely break even. We had too many cows that were unprofitable with milk at only $3.55 per hundredweight, but Dad so desperately needed the cash flow that he felt he dared not get rid of the poorer ones. We argued vehemently about it and about many other things. I learned—oh, how I learned—that fast expansion in farming (in any business) was disastrous no matter how the numbers crunched on paper. I saw it in our operation; I saw it in others. Nature does not read agricultural economists' calculations. And corn grows by its own natural rhythms, not by the demands of money interest. It was obvious to me that even though there was work for even another person, one of us had to get off the payroll for awhile, and since I was the unmarried one, why not me? All we were doing, although it was not then clear to me, was testing and perfecting the technology that, in twenty years, would allow factory farms with outside investment money to swallow us up.

Jimmy Downs called up one day. He was for sure going to the air force and had to sell his car. Having opened my mouth, I did not now want to lose face. And I had saved enough money to buy it. Besides . . . "Yes," he laughed, "I still think you might have to take Carol in the bargain."

The year 1958 turned into 1959. Other than the convertible, which I had bought for a reason so madly preposterous that I would not admit it even to myself, I spent money only when I could not avoid doing so. Looking neither to the right nor left, I saved every penny to buy my "someday farm," as I called it, even if it were only ten acres.

But in January 1960, I decided to take a few days off and go by train to Minnesota to Donny's ordination to the priesthood. I was curious about what had happened to Yellow Rose, and I was sure Carol would be there.

Minnesota worked its magic once again. Doc, who was still in charge of things, offered me a room at the seminary. We tried to pretend that our previous battle of wills was a bit of a joke between us now, but neither of us had much to say on that subject. I could hardly tell him that he had inadvertently convinced me that men create their gods, not vice versa. As I settled in for the night, thinking how strange it was to be back here under such different circumstances, Donny stuck his head in the door and said, "Let's sneak down to the priests' rec room and steal some beer," just as if it were five years earlier and we were still students. We both laughed. He wanted me to come on downstairs and meet his family, who had just arrived from Kentucky.

I walked into the room where all the Downses sat. Even before I could greet the parents formally, I heard from the far side of the room a familiar, playful Kentucky drawl.

"Where's my Bluebird?"

I spun around to see what seemed to me the most stunningly beautiful woman in all the world coming toward me. Carol? Could it be Donny's little sister, now emerged from the chrysalis of girlhood into a radiant butterfly of womanhood?

"*Your* Bluebird?" I replied, trying to sound cool and debonair. Mentally I cursed myself for taking the train instead of driving. "I don't remember getting any donations when I was paying for it."

She put her hands on her hips, feigning petulance. "That was *my* car, and you went and bought it, you, you, *scrub*."

Was I the only one who could hear the electricity snapping

through the air between us? I could not talk, could hardly breathe. I tried to smile. She smiled back. And I knew.

The ordination was only a fog of incense and ritual. But I noted every move that Carol made for the next two days. By the time we had wined and dined and danced at the Shakopee Inn at the end of the celebration, I was in a trance. How could something this strangely wonderful be happening to me? I led her by the hand to the window in the restaurant.

"Do you believe in magic?" I asked.

"Nope."

"I do," I said. When she didn't react, I continued. "Do you know that the early settlers, while dining in this restaurant, once watched two tribes of Indians battle right over there across the river? Maybe right from this very room."

"You're lying, you scrub."

"No, really."

She stared at me, eyes dancing, still not quite believing. "Well, here's some more magic for you. Once when I was a little girl, I was looking out the window of our house at our old potato barn, and it collapsed. No wind or nothing. It just smack-dab gave up in a heap while I was watching. Like maybe my eyes did it." She grinned wickedly. "That put an end to Daddy making bootleg in there."

I could not quit laughing, even after we went back to the dance floor. "You sure you don't believe in magic?" I asked again.

Our eyes met. "Maybe," she said.

Back home, I got a letter from her. She wanted me to come to see her. I walked dreamlike through my work, bumping into barn doors, forgetting to turn on the silo unloader to feed the cows, then forgetting to turn it off until Dad yelled that the bunk was overflowing. I would let the cows into one side of the milking parlor, then absent-mindedly let them out without milking them. I was dangerous to work around, my brother said. As soon as I could get free, I drove to Louisville. Everything that I hoped was true, came true.

The fellowship from Indiana University that magically came

my way would never have happened either were it not indirectly because of Carol. I decided to finish up regular undergraduate studies at Bellarmine College in Louisville, not because I really cared about getting a degree but because I wanted an excuse to be near her. I even thought that after we married, I'd go back and rejoin my father at the home farm, although economics was rapidly making that impossible. But had I not gone to Bellarmine, I would never have seen the notice posted on the bulletin board about the National Defense Education Act grants in what was termed "American Studies: Folklore" being offered by Indiana University. I applied on a whim (Indiana University was not far from Louisville and not terribly far from home in Ohio). I was nearly struck dumb when I was selected for one of the fellowships.

"What's 'American Studies: Folklore'?" Carol wanted to know when I told her.

"I'm not sure," I replied, and that was the truth.

"Well, how did you get it?"

"I have no idea," I said.

"But how can you get a fellowship that pays $3,000 a year when you don't even know anything about it?" she asked, wrinkling up her face in mystification.

"Magic," I said, "Now we can get married."

○

Anything seemed possible now that Carol had come into my life. Even being able to rent the idyllic log cabin in the woods just a mile from the university had been a stroke of luck that I could not explain. I had walked unknown into a real estate office and told the kindly old broker sitting there eyeing me quizzically that I was hoping to rent cheaply a little house in the country near Bloomington. He smiled and said there was no such thing. We talked awhile, during which I told him about Carol and me being from the farm and how we hated apartments, especially now with a child and a second on the way. He kept asking questions, seeming to be resolving something in his mind. When I started to leave, he abruptly told me about his own country place, a log cabin in the woods, which he was not in good enough health to take care of anymore. Right there on the spot he decided we could rent it and rent it cheaply. Magic.

Playing with the kids in the pile of leaves Carol and I had raked up in the front yard, I wondered if anyone could be luckier than I and at the same time more frustrated. We were poor by financial standards, true enough, but we lived in a beautiful grove of trees surrounded by the pasture fields of a wealthy man's farm estate, hardly a mile from the university. The five-acre grove was mostly old-growth forest. Huge black walnut, wild cherry, beech, oak, and tulip poplar trees towered over the property with a sprinkle of birch, butternut, hickory, sassafras, and persimmon wherever sunlight permitted. In spring, an array of wildflowers spread over the woodland dell,— extensive patches of bluebells and buttercups in the ravine behind the cabin; Quaker ladies, violets, and spring beauties in the lawn in front; firepink and hepatica in the deep shade of the old growth forest; shooting stars and trilliums climbing the hill beyond the ravine. Walnuts, hickory nuts, butternuts, and beechnuts littered the ground in the fall. Morel mushrooms popped up in spring. Bird-song filled the air in all seasons.

But being too poor and dislocated to own my own land was beating me down. At night I walked alone around the property, fretting, possessed with the idea of just throwing caution to the wind and following in the footsteps of Harlan and Anna Hubbard, whom I'd just learned about. They lived across the Ohio River from Madison, Indiana, and had perfected an almost completely self-sufficient life. They had no electricity, heated their owner-built home entirely with their own wood, raised all their food, did not own an automobile, and got by with a little cash Harlan made from painting pictures. For entertainment they played the piano and violin, read books, and studied the natural happenings around them. They lived an elegant life without much modern technology. I was totally taken. Why couldn't we do likewise? The lifestyle of the Hubbards might be the *only* way we could ever have our own true home. I talked incessantly of following their example. But our parents and relatives replied with stony silence, and even Carol was hesitant. There were the children, you see. I was sure the children would be better off and better educated in that environment, but it was not an argument I could win. I bowed my head, ground my teeth, and paced in the moonlight.

One night when we put the kids to bed, Jerry, age one, seemed a bit fussier than his sister, Jenny, a year older. At about midnight, he awoke, crying and coughing hoarsely. In the space of only a few minutes, he was having difficulty breathing. Carol grabbed the phone but could not get in touch with our doctor. The nurse at the hospital said she'd keep trying. Jerry's breathing became more labored.

"He's got the croup, I think," Carol said.

"Is that bad?" I asked. I thought croup was some old wives' holdover from pioneer days, perhaps appropriate since snow sometimes sifted through the cracks in the chinking of our log cabin.

Jerry started to gasp. I panicked. Should we get him to the hospital? Where *was* the nearest hospital anyway?

"I don't think there's time," Carol said, grabbing the teakettle. She filled it and set it on the stove to boil.

"What are you doing?" I asked, wild-eyed by now.

"Steam. That's what they did in that movie *Song of the South*. It's the croup and steam relieves it."

I felt numb and dumb, like a wart, useless and in the way in this time of crisis. As Jerry's breathing grew alarmingly worse, I thought he was going to die right in our arms. But Carol was all fiery action, rolling him, pushing on his little lungs, keeping the throat open just a little. He gagged, fought the constriction, vomited. That cleared the air passages just enough for him to suck in a little oxygen and gain us a little more time. The teakettle sang. Carol held the poor baby as close to the cloud of steam as she dared. Miraculously, his labored breath came easier. All three of us were trembling. The phone rang. It was Dr. Link. Thank God.

"Get him in here right away," he said after hearing our story.

Carol stayed home with Jenny, and I drove like a maniac through the dark, Jerry beside me on the car seat. But I knew the crisis had passed. He just whimpered now, looking at me in that heart-tugging, bewildered way of sick children who can't understand what's happening to them.

Dr. Link gave him a shot of adrenaline and we sat in his office awhile to see if another attack was forthcoming. I liked Link because he ministered to the poor people in the grim ghetto on Pigeon Hill even though he knew he'd never get paid adequately. Pigeon Hill, on the opposite side of Bloomington from the comfortable community of Indiana University, was steeped in venereal disease, malnutrition, inbreeding, and poverty. Pigeon Hill and the university, less than a mile apart, were as different as the black holes of Calcutta were from the serenity of the Taj Mahal. I knew about Pigeon Hill because, in the ultimate show of hypocrisy and hauteur, I, the folklore collector from the university, went there, not to help these people, but to rob them of their last shred of nobility, their dying rural culture. Link and I talked about that. He nodded. He understood.

"Is there any hope for people like that?" I asked. "As a matter of fact, is there any hope for a world where society accepts extreme wealth and extreme poverty existing side by side?"

"I've thought about it a lot," he said. "I know it isn't possible, but the only solution I can come up with is to give everyone ten acres of land which they could never sell or never add to, and then make them provide their own food, clothing, and shelter—or die trying. I think we'd be surprised at how much better the world would do under those circumstances."

Of all the things I learned at the university, that idea impressed me the most. Impractical and impossible, no doubt, but it became the philosophy behind my determination to establish my homestead, to get back home in the truest sense.

A week later, Jerry was running and tumbling with Jenny outside the cabin door as if nothing had happened to him. The front lawn had once been landscaped with stone benches, which still remained, and with formal gardens that had turned ragged with unpruned shrubbery, intruding wild blackberry canes, and tree seedlings. I had cleaned it all up. Though rough and somewhat primitive, the log cabin had indoor plumbing, a cistern for water, electricity, and an oil furnace, with a huge fireplace for backup heat and cooking. We maintained a big garden and derived our recreation from our homestead, so our cost of living in cash was small. Chicken wings were eleven cents a pound and pork chops nineteen cents. Carol was calm and capable, a born mother, as she had proven with Jerry's croup. She was as content to be home with the children as I was. I never heard her fret, except over the skunks that often stank up the air around the cabin in spring and the snake that once appeared on the stairsteps.

A creek ran through the property, which we splashed in with the kids on summer days. There was a spring next to the creek below the house, and rusting pipes indicated that at one time the artesian flow had had enough pressure to rise to the cabin providing running water without pumps. I itched to restore the piping and see if the spring could again be harnessed that way, but not owning the property, I could not.

"If only we could buy this place," I sighed to Carol. "If only I could somehow work right here and make a living and turn this place into a self-sufficient little paradise."

"It *is* that," Carol said.

"Not nearly what it could be if I owned it. Will we ever be able to have a place like this of our own?" I was trying to bring her around to my Hubbard way of thinking, but she was too sensible.

"Wherever you get a job will be home," she said.

"But I won't be there most of the time," I protested. "I'll be away all the time making the goddam money. I can't stand the thought of that."

"You'll figure out a way," she said.

I was trying to do just that. If it took a Ph.D. to get a grub-stake so we could go back to home land, so be it. I'd become a professor of something and use my teaching career as a front for a private life of subsistence farming. I would spend my fellowship time earning a doctorate in ornery knowledge.

The first year our tomatoes were hardly the size of golf balls, our beans sulked in too much shade, and our corn barely grew shoulder high. But we were learning. Just as I studied farming more than theology in the seminary, so now I studied subsistence living more than American Studies. Subsistent living WAS American Studies. I read everything I could get my hands on about unusual homesteading activities such as growing mushrooms, raising fish-worms and chinchillas, keeping bees, breeding exotic, endangered livestock species—any possibility of making money at home no matter how seemingly impractical. Because I had no money to put into such ventures, I avoided the embarrassment of losing any and earned instead a degree in practical, everyday, frugal living.

Because of my nonacademic background, I was fascinated by university life. The students often reminded me of ants scurrying over an anthill in a paroxysm of busyness. They were all so terribly earnest in their firm belief that they were ensuring themselves perfect financial security for the future. In a society which believed that the Christian God was the only God, the belief, for all practical purposes, became fact. Likewise, in a society which believed that a college degree was the necessary road to earthly riches, the myth became fact. Institutional religion's terrible power to bestow heavenly salvation was then matched by institutional education's terrible power to bestow financial salvation. Who would not pay whatever tribute necessary to be so blessed?

My fellowship was the most mystifying blessedness of all, coming as it did through the National Defense Education Act. What did studying folklore and folk music have to do with national defense? I tried to picture us storming the Berlin Wall with drawn guitars.

One of my part-time jobs could not even have been imagined

by milkers of cows. I became a folklore archivist. On 3-by-5-inch cards, I indexed and cataloged traditional beliefs, superstitions, songs, jokes, folktales, proverbs, and other types of oral lore that had been collected by students taking the introductory course in Folklore. Among these bits of recorded folklore were some of the bawdiest songs and lewdest expressions I'd ever heard anywhere, even in milking parlors. I always thought a friend of mine from Wisconsin had invented the expression "a piss-complected puddle of puke," but there it was showing up on cards from South Dakota. And that was a milder example. I often found myself hunched over the table, convulsed in stifled laughter. At other times I simply smiled over the irony of finding myself, for all practical purposes a farm boy or a woodland savage who read too much, in such strange circumstances. I wondered what American taxpayers would think had they known what their taxes were funding.

Often the head of the Folklore Institute and head of my doctoral committee, Richard Dorson, would be in the room where I "worked," because he maintained an office there. Dorson was a good-natured, jocular sort of fellow on the outside, but shrewd, intensely ambitious, and extremely hard-working on the inside. He never approved of me wholeheartedly, as if he sensed the unscholarly and irreverent soul lurking within me. But he was "a study," as my grandfather would have said. He would arrive at his desk on the dead run with his clothes in disarray, totally ignoring me. One day when he removed his suit coat, as he habitually did before attacking one of his books in progress, I could see his shirt was badly torn. It was held together by a huge safety pin. His long-suffering secretary, who took care of his earthly concerns, scolded him mildly for his unkempt appearance, but he only grunted, jabbing away with his pencil at the infinitives and participles that dared to split and dangle before him.

"Don't you think you ought to buy a new shirt or two?" she suggested, bending directly into his ear to get his attention.

"Mmmfff. Not a bad idea," he responded, nose still in the manuscript. "Here, go downtown and get some right now." He extended his billfold without taking his eyes off the misplaced modifiers that were creeping stealthily through his manuscript. "While you're at it, might as well buy a whole suit."

"W-what size?" she asked, eyes bulging.

"Oh, I don't know. Forty-two, maybe. Call my wife. She knows."

I also worked for awhile in the museum of History, Anthropology and Folklore. I got paid for doing fascinating things like reconstructing prehistoric clay pots, using plaster of paris to fill in the missing pieces. One part of my duties allowed me to fulfill a long-time ambition: I went to farm sales, buying old and folkloric artifacts of farming for the museum. After years of attending auctions on my own and being too poor to buy much, I could stand there and impertinently outbid rich old dowagers buying farm "antiques" to decorate their homes—tools that would not be "antique" if the economic system that produced rich old dowagers had not destroyed the rural society that used them and with them made the wealth that the dowagers inherited. Outbidding them gave me a tremendous feeling. Peasant revenge. I had the whole state of Indiana behind me.

Another job found me counting cars and people entering Spring Mill State Park. There I stood before the incoming tourists, once more overwhelmed by the drollery of the situation. I, the ex-milker of cows, ex-theologian of obtuse Catholic dogma, ex-digger of tile ditches, ex-cataloger of dirty jokes, was now Chief Car Counter for the Proud State of Indiana. I applied for the job without much hope because it came through the Recreation and Physical Education department, not American Studies. Carol figured that I got it because the Recreation students were too busy recreating to have time to count cars. The reason for counting cars had something to do with future plans for expanding camping grounds in the state parks. The fact that people wanted to buy expensive campers and flee their nice suburban homes for crowded campgrounds in a state park struck me as something doctoral candidates in abnormal psychology should have been interested in, not the Recreation department.

But mine was not to reason why. I worked at these jobs because I had to. I felt only a deep and dire frustration because all those hours and days of my life ticking by were forever lost to my goal of developing my own homestead farm.

The three years of fellowship money came to an end, but I still needed another year to complete my dissertation. Our poverty now became critical. A full-time teaching position in Folklore, for which I was presumably preparing myself, was not available anywhere until my doctoral work was complete, and even then it was not assured. In the meantime, I taught a class at the Kokomo branch. I kept working in the museum. I borrowed a thousand dollars. I learned with shock that some of my associates, grown men and women, were getting monthly checks from home to keep them going. No way could I do that. I began to suspect that the Ph.D. was the property of the upper classes.

"Why don't you try to write and sell stuff to magazines?" Carol asked, more than once.

"You want us to starve to death for sure?" I answered. I had often talked about writing for a living, but I had little confidence that I could sell anything.

She stared at me. "Everybody knows that's what you should do except you. Do you know that?"

"How can you be so sure?" Certitude always amazed me.

"I just know."

"What in the world could I write that anybody would buy?"

"Write something funny."

"Whaaat?"

"Write something funny about farming. That's what you know."

"The world's too pathetic for that."

"Write something funny."

There was a second, tiny cabin on our homestead, so I cleaned it out and turned it into a writing place, like real writers were supposed to have. There I sat, trying to think of something wise to expound upon. Little daughter Jenny toddled in constantly, demanding that I play with her. And I did. The writing pad remained empty. Finally, I bowed to Carol's suggestion and tried to write something funny. At least that made the pencil move. I wrote something about pipe smoking becoming a rage with women. Terrible. I wrote a futuristic piece about a time when clothes were outlawed and naked students rioted, demanding the right to garb themselves, and spinners and weavers hid out in the woods like moonshiners, operating illegal spinning wheels and looms. Too farfetched. In desperation, I started writing about amusing things that happened on the farm at home. That was easy. I wrote about how, if something as innocent as an old bucket got left in the barnyard, it would shortly attract more trash to it like a magnet, until a month later, the spot would festoon into a miniature junkyard. I sent it to *Farm Journal*, the only farm magazine I had ever read much.

Magic. A check for $200 came back. I sent in another piece about how cows had varying personalities just like humans. A check for $250 came back. Another quick piece brought $150—about how we lived in a chaos of lost tools on the home farm because none of us could discipline ourselves to put anything away.

The heavens were opening up and raining down gold. I figured I could write this trivia by the bushel and get rich.

"I told you so," Carol said.

A few months later, a *Farm Journal* editor in Philadelphia dropped over dead at his desk. I never knew him, of course, but I wonder if all that followed would ever have happened if he had possessed a stronger heart. At about the same time, the *Wall Street Journal* reprinted one of my humor pieces from *Farm Journal*. The *Farm Journal* editors, I would later learn, thought *WSJ* was God's own daily bulletin, and by and by I was asked if I wanted to take the dead man's place. I replied immediately in the affirmative. Here was my first real chance to get back home. I would work at *Farm Journal* until I learned enough to become an independent writer and then go find home.

So my plot to become a professor by day and a contrary farmer by sundown came to an abrupt end. By leaving the university system, I alienated myself from it just as I alienated myself from the Church. I never did get a Ph.D. No man is master of his fate, or gets where he goes purely on his own decisions. We all float along on whims of chance, like thistledown on an August breeze.

CHAPTER *5/* *Suburban Halfway House*

I was gripping the steering wheel with such force that my arms ached to my shoulders. If the car stalled, if for any reason I were detained on this bleak and empty street that was too far gone to even be called a ghetto, I was sure I'd be attacked, killed, robbed, my car stripped, dismantled, carried away. I would disappear from the face of the earth. No one—not even Carol—knew where I was. *I* did not know where I was except somewhere in Philadelphia. I had driven off the turnpike with the idea of taking State Route 309 into downtown. I became confused, having never tried to negotiate really heavy traffic before, and had gotten off on a wrong street. When I finally realized I was lost, I took the first street south, judging by the sun, knowing that as long as I continued in that direction, I would, according to the map, eventually run into Walnut Street or Market Street or, if not, into Delaware Bay. On Market Street, I could then find my way to the hotel where the *Farm Journal* editors were having their annual meeting.

I was reading the Philadelphia map as I would have interpreted a map of my home village, that is, without understanding how unimaginably big the city was. In my village conceptualization of urban reality, taking any street to Main Street would work out, and since I was already "in town," the ride would be fairly short.

That bit of fanciful thinking had occurred what seemed like

an hour ago, and I was now driving in terror through block after block of rubble, deserted buildings, and gutted hulks of cars along the curb. No shops or gas stations. No churches, except one with the front door missing and all the windows boarded up. No schools, no theaters, no apartments, not even a bar. I tried to read street signs. Some were missing. It occurred to me that others might have been changed so as to lure a stranger into mazes of concrete jungle and be swallowed up forever. I just kept going straight. The sun, hardly visible through the sky's haze, said I was still headed south, more or less.

I could not believe that such a large area of dead city could exist in the United States. At one point I saw a pair of eyes peering out at me through a sagging door from the dark interior of a building. The eyes reminded me of a raccoon staring out of a hollow tree. Pigeon Hill, back in Bloomington, was squalid, but it was a populated squalor in which people lived openly, unafraid at least of each other, where a stranger might feel safe to walk or at least drive through. Here the whole scene struck me as terrifyingly sinister. There were no children playing in the streets even though it was a warm day. There were no women about either—just a few seedy old men slouching along. Wind-driven boxes and newspapers rolled across the street like tumbleweeds in a Hollywood ghost town. There was no traffic, which, I realized, was the main reason the place seemed so eerie. If a street gang wanted to take me down, there were no passing cars to deter them.

How could an area that seemed bigger than my whole home village have declined so drastically? No war or plague could have done a better job. And this was once part of William Penn's "greene countrie town."

Stopped at a red light, I noticed a group of young men materialize and start walking toward me, testily yet slowly, figuring, I hoped, that no one with an Ohio license plate would be fool enough to come onto their turf—that the car must be stolen and its driver heavily armed. I hit the accelerator and never stopped for a red light after that. I yearned for the company of a law officer.

Eventually I did come to more habitable surroundings and finally to Market Street. For the first and only time, I found the horrendous traffic jam I now encountered heavenly by contrast to the wasteland I had escaped. Finally, by what seemed to me a miracle, I found the Holiday Inn. The rest of the afternoon, I listened to *Farm Journal* editors talk earnestly about the problems of agriculture, as if oblivious to the hell that festered not twenty minutes from their comfortable hotel rooms.

I often asked Philadelphians I worked with about my terrifying drive on my first day there: were my fears grounded, or was I just seeing ghetto reality for the first time and suffering cultural shock? The usual answer was "Uh, no one in his right mind goes *into* there"—"into" seeming to refer to a totally different planet than Mother Earth. When I questioned further about where "into" was located exactly, and what it might be called other than some general nod toward "north Philly," it was apparent that none of these white, middle-class urbanites had ever been where I had been. And some even doubted what I described.

I never drove into center city again, but rode the train every work day, first in fear that I might miss my station and lose my way, for I had never ridden a city bus, subway, or railway before, and later in growing dismal frustration. I hated the clamor, the seemingly pointless bustle, the dense diesel bus fumes downtown, the air that even in parks smelled stale. When the trains were delayed, as they often were, hundreds of us would get squeezed together in the old Reading Terminal, waiting for our rides. The indignity of having no private space around me, bodies mashed together like so many sheep in a shearing shed, generated in me a glowering, gritty anger. I swore under my breath that I would beat the wage-slavocracy that chained me to the city and escape. My anger kept me writing. I would write my way back to open country. But I didn't know if I could do that. How did a person know when he was writing something good? Was good writing what would sell? I decided good writing was whatever got me back to the land, far from this wretched city. In the meantime, I learned about editors. Knowing editors was more important to my purposes. Poor writers with families to feed did not write for themselves, nor for readers, nor for the ages. We wrote for editors.

The only problem was that when I tried not to write for myself, I could not write much at all.

In my first conversation with Carroll Streeter and Lane Palmer, the editor and managing editor at *Farm Journal*, Streeter asked me why I had come to work for him. I almost said that no one else was crazy enough to pay me $10,000 a year to do anything, let alone write. But instead I declared that I wanted to learn how to be a writer, which was also true. Streeter did not appear impressed.

"Do you think you can get excited writing stories about calf scours?" he asked dryly. I did not know whether a smile was appropriate at what seemed to me an outlandish question. I had been warned that Streeter could be a dragon. But I grinned anyway. The years in the seminary had made me utterly devoid of fear of authoritarian power.

"Don't know why not," I answered. "Most everything written is bullshit of one kind or another." Out of the corner of my eye, I saw Palmer duck his head. I wasn't trying to be clever. Or bold. I was just saying what popped into my nervous mind.

Streeter looked surprised, but recovered quickly.

"Do you like what you read in our magazine?"

"Some of your editorials are too conservative, I think." I was back in the seminary again, saying the wrong things because I was too flustered to lie.

A faint flush of red came into his neck. But then to my great relief, he grinned. I could tell he kind of liked people stupid enough to say what they were really thinking.

"Plenty of magazines are bleating the liberal point of view, so I aim to balance the score," he rasped in his gravelly editorial voice.

"The *New Yorker* is my favorite magazine," I said, not so much to argue with him, but because it was just the truth. I couldn't help it.

He sniffed. "Nobody reads those long articles. A good editor would cut out half the words and not lose a thing." Palmer nodded in agreement.

I turned my head to look out the window, not trusting my expression to their full view. What the hell had I gotten myself into? How was I going to learn how to write from editors who repudiated what I thought was some of the best prose being published in the English language?

My *Farm Journal* mentors did, however, teach me precious lessons of brevity and clarity. The trouble was that I would not practice the lessons unless absolutely forced to. When I tried to write in the brief, just-the-facts way they taught, my copy sounded to me like cereal-box rhetoric. I couldn't change the basic way my mind transferred thought to paper without deliberate and painful effort, sort of like pricking myself repeatedly with a dull knife. Once, going through a drawer full of saved memorabilia, I discovered two old magazines from the seminary in which I had written adolescent short stories. Although they were awful, of course, to my amazement my basic writing style had been established by the time I was sixteen years old! That was me, to fail or succeed. Not even Streeter and Palmer, two of the most resolute taskmasters I'd ever known, could change that. I learned after awhile to submit my copy for scourging a little after deadline when I wanted to preserve my own identity in my writing. Then the editorial grinding committee didn't have time to rewrite my copy to blend with what they referred to as the "*Farm Journal* Way."

Sometimes Streeter, Palmer, and Dick Davids, the only liberal on the staff, expressed philosophical disagreement over what I had written. Davids, who had "discovered" me, became my chief mentor in journalistic instruction. He would tilt my copy a bit more toward the liberal ideology he believed in and thought I should. Joe Dan Boyd, the assistant managing editor and the only kindly person in the editing process, would change all the passive verbs to active ones no matter what and rehang the modifying phrases in their proper places. Palmer, next up the ladder of editorial browbeating, would scratch out David's tilting and insert his own, more conservative fix on the subject, which he thought that I, being a reasonable person like himself, would surely go along with. Streeter would slash furiously away at all the edits and my original copy with his pencil stub, sometimes stabbing right through three or four carbons to make his point. His point was often scrawled in the margin: "What the hell does this mean to a farmer?"

The editors were all originally farm boys like myself, and I got along well with them, even the most conservative hidebinders. Considering how inexperienced I was in everyday journalism, their patience with my flights of rhetorical fancy was remarkable. Boyd, who would later win almost all the top awards that agricultural journalism offered, was the person who taught me the most. He was closer to my age and understood the struggle I was going through. I didn't really want to write about production agriculture. I wanted to write about people in all their quirks and he empathized with that urge. We became friends, although we were very different in personality. He was reserved and cautious; I was outspoken and reckless. But once he invited me to a country music jamboree far out beyond the reach of the city. Farmland surrounded the little country park where real bluegrass and country music singers had gathered. In this environment Joe was transformed into a different person—outgoing, jocular, completely relaxed, a big cigar in his mouth. He insisted I smoke one too. To my surprise, he knew some of the singers, played the ukelele, and sang well himself. He was an authority on country and western music. In the office, one would never have guessed.

After several years, he finally revealed to me that he shared my conspiracy about going home again.

"Joe, what the hell is a farm magazine doing in Philadelphia?" I complained to him. "I hate cities. How can we write well about farmers if we don't live with them?"

He looked amused. "Well, our families are all farmers. We were raised on farms. We understand the culture. I will always be a Texan."

"Well, I'll always be a midwesterner. Don't tell anyone, but I'm going back home as soon as I can save the money."

He looked at me for a minute or two without speaking. Then he almost whispered, as if afraid he might be overheard, "Me too."

But commuting into Philadelphia every day taught me a valuable lesson about urban culture too. I began to understand what kept large cities from flying apart in the sort of centrifugal force that the stress and strain of dense population generated. I had fallen into the habit of walking through a Greek neighborhood on the way from train station to office. Just a few minutes from seething center city, this community seemed settled and quiet and made me feel at home. It was in fact a village in every respect, but invisible as such to the casual eye because it was surrounded by city. I would stop in a little family bakery there and buy a certain sweet roll that I had grown fond of. One morning I missed, and when I again showed up, the matriarch of the family, who always ran the cash register, looked up and, for the first time ever, spoke to me: "Where were you yesterday?" I was taken aback. In a city of three million people, I'd been missed, just as I would have been missed in little Upper Sandusky back home. And then I understood. Big cities were much more than the hubs of big business, big museums, big sports stadiums, big hotels, big shopping centers, big airports, and big factories. What kept a big city viable and sane were the individual human neighborhoods that glued it together.

I was finally hammered and shaped into a farm journalist of sorts. But I could never quite be in harmony with the editors. My guitar strings just weren't tuned to theirs. I was not sired by agribusiness out of land grant colleges. *Farm Journal* was not the top of the agricultural wave for me, much less the journalistic wave. I had learned the dark and dirty side of agribusiness from a hundred cows pissing and shitting down on me in a modern milking pit, not from an agricultural economist in a nice, comfortable classroom. I knew that large-scale farming was a money game, like writing copy to fill the blank pages between advertisements. Neither had much to do with the human artfulness that I was seeking.

My original plan at *Farm Journal* was to combine small-scale farming with writing. To my chagrin I learned that any small farm within commuting distance of Philadelphia was millionaire property. A person had to be rich to enjoy the kind of poor sharecropping environment I grew up in. Even trying to buy five or ten acres with a house was out of the question for us.

So Carol and I did the next best thing. We bought a small house with two acres and pretended it was a farm. Used to the five acres in Bloomington, and to several hundred acres back home, I was delightfully surprised at how large two acres could be when gardened intensively. I slowly realized that with very skillful horticulture, a family could produce almost all its food on two acres, or indeed one acre. In fact there was potential on that much land to supply several families with fruit, vegetables, fowl, eggs, and possibly fish. I learned about Italian immigrants in south Philadelphia who raised all their fruit, vegetables, chickens, rabbits, and a goat for milk on lots of scarcely one hundred feet by two hundred feet including the house. And some made wine for the whole neighborhood to boot. This discovery electrified me. I did not necessarily have to have a farm in the conventional sense to live the kind of life I desired. A couple of acres could be a life-fulfilling challenge. Human civilization could feed itself with a multitude of backyard-garden farms as China and Japan had done for centuries.

I turned inwardly upon our place, as if it were the whole world. This was the first time in my life that I possessed my very own land, and I was surprised none of my colleagues thought this was exciting. What could be more revolutionary than to pursue a self-subsistent life right in the middle of suburbia? Never once did I go to the office early or stay late. I rendered to Caesar the bare minimum of time and rendered to myself and my family the rest of it. While others fled to the ocean or the mountains on weekends and in the evenings partook of the cultural treats that the city provided, Carol and I stayed home with our children, saved our money, and made a life for ourselves in what other people called the boring suburbs—just as an earlier generation had called rural life boring. With a thick hedge on both sides of our property, a little woodlot behind it, and similar backyards on either side of us, we enjoyed more privacy and solitude than we had known in the farm country of the Midwest and a more relaxing place to recreate than trying to drive traffic-jammed highways to vacation resorts. On weekends we hiked through the valley of Wissahickon Creek nearby, through estates of rich people who were invariably very hospitable to us. I had a hunch we enjoyed their property more than they did. We gathered hickory nuts, fished, hunted Indian artifacts, picked wild berries, dug antique glass bottles out of long abandoned dumps, tobogganed the nearby hills, skated the creek, bicycled the back roads. We lived in fact, as we had always lived. I even found a softball team to play on.

We developed a food-or-fiber plan for every square foot of our property. We raised chickens and rabbits and a full complement of fruits and vegetables, constantly adding to the knowledge we had gained at the log cabin. If I could grow it, Carol could preserve it. Two of our neighbors kept chickens and big gardens too, so we did not feel culturally isolated. There was a hint of real community among us. It was clear to me that my vision of a nation of garden farms was altogether practical if the will of society turned to, or was forced to turn to, that direction. We were halfway home.

Then another "coincidence" occurred that made me wonder if I were following a script already written for me. I found *Organic Gardening* magazine, which was espousing the same gardening vision that was taking hold of me, a vision that would allow it to blossom into a major magazine. I went to see Bob Rodale, the editor, since the magazine was headquartered only about thirty miles north of our suburban homestead. He said everything about the future of food production that I believed but had been afraid to say out loud. "The typical farm of the future may very well be just a very large garden," he said.

Eventually, I started writing a few "backyard farming" articles for him, which did not sit well at *Farm Journal* and which might have meant job suicide for me since the philosophies of the two magazine were opposed to each other—chemical vs. organic. But as usual, my "mistake" turned out to be most fortunate.

I was starting to hate my job, as wonderful as it must have looked to most people and really would have been for most journalists. I commuted daily into the big city, where I felt the pulse and thrum of so-called social progress. I had an expense account that allowed me to jump on an airplane and fly anywhere in the nation in pursuit of society's most vital news: information about food production. I lived in comfortable, middle-class suburban surroundings. No one could be better informed from his "environment." Yet contrarily, I was vastly dissatisfied. I hated to travel, for one thing. I hated not being at home. Once I was gone for two weeks and when I got back, little Jerry hardly recognized me. Sometimes on the road, I grew so melancholy that I just sat in my motel room and cried. Back home I might lay on the couch half a day in enervating depression because I knew I would soon have to travel again.

I also hated interviewing farmers about making money—asking questions I already knew the answers to or were none of my business. I got little satisfaction out of writing breezy, shallow stories about people that I had not known the week before and would never meet again. I wanted to live in one place deeply, write in solitude, think more slowly. I understood, fearfully, that I was not a journalist at all, that I was acting a part again, as in the seminary and university, waiting patiently for the curtain to fall. Would I be found out and lose my job, the only financial security we possessed?

Ω

"There's something good about cities after all," I said to Carol as we toured the exhibit of Andrew Wyeth paintings at the Philadelphia Museum of Art. "They're the only places that can afford to do this."

"Even though most city people can't afford to partake of it," she replied.

I had never cared much about any paintings before, but Wyeth was different. He saw rural America like I did. When I read what he said about the creative process, I became so excited I thought my skin was going to rip apart. Here finally was something about creativity I could understand and apply directly to my writing. His great paintings were done within walking distances of the places where he lived. *He stayed at home.* He emphasized the necessity of knowing a place deeply to draw art from it, of "living deeply the thing that nourished you." A precise act of art depended on seeing the fleeting moment of a happening. That moment could not be contrived. "Pictures happen; you don't sit down and make them up," he said.

That was true of writing, too. You had to be at the right place and time to catch it, either by luck or from living in one place continuously over a long period of time so that you could recognize the *magic* moment. You had to put down roots in a place. News journalism only skimmed off the froth.

I had to talk to Wyeth, a most difficult challenge since it was harder to get an audience with him than with the pope. But I was driven and finally, partly by accident, I met him in a little diner at Chadds Ford and we talked for an hour. That meeting led to a story, which Streeter, bless him, ran in the magazine even though it was not "news that mattered to farmers." (It mattered to farmers a whole lot more than all that tripe about making money.) That article led to my writing a book, thanks to the support of Gertrude Dieken, a highly placed editor at *Farm Journal*, about the people whom Wyeth painted. Though the book made little money, the act of writing it was a great comfort to my spirit. That was a kind of writing that I wanted to do all the time.

Then I ran across a little book of poetry called *Farming: A Hand Book*, by Wendell Berry, which affected me in the same way that Wyeth's paintings had. I went to see Berry and wrote an article about him too. Almost all of his inspiration he drew from his own farm and community in the Kentucky hills. He had gone back home from the glitter of New York to make his own solitary way.

And so, I vowed, would I.

Next I was able to write a book about gardening on our suburban homestead. It did not sell well either, but the spark ignited something. I got a call one day from Lee Goldman at Rodale Press.

"Your last article was well received," he said. "Would you be interested in doing a book for us? About modern homesteading. As you described in your last piece. We can get off an advance of $2500 if that's okay."

I almost swooned. Did he say okay? Lord, I'd have done it for no advance.

"Wow. Okay. Sure," I replied. And just like that the book was commissioned, without an agent, without signing any long, lawyer-worded agreement or contract, without my submitting a stuffy proposal or attending an even stuffier planning meeting. Magic.

I could hardly imagine being asked to write a book about what I did in my spare time. I did not let myself think about what would happen if it were not financially successful either. I pounded it out at night while working for *Farm Journal* during the day. Jenny and Jerry grew jealous of my typewriter.

One lovely day about a year later, a Saturday, Carol and I were busy in the garden when I decided to go get the mail. The Gwynedd post office was near our home and walking there through the empty lot, woodlot, and Quaker Friends cemetery behind our gardens was one of our semi-rural treats. I returned at a leisurely pace, enjoying the walk, not bothering to examine the parcels until I had reached our property again. There was a letter from Rodale Press. I opened it, took one look, and sank down weakly under the pin oak tree half way up the garden path.

"What's the matter?" Carol asked, dropping her hoe and walking quickly over to me.

"We just broke free, honey. By God we did." I handed her the check. It was for over $5,000, the first royalty check from the book, an enormous amount to us. "We're going home."

She looked at the check, beamed, and said, "See, I told you you could do it."

I stared at her. "If we go home, it has to be with the idea that we'll be happy even if the best job I can get is driving a feedmill truck," I said. "Can you handle that?"

She smiled. "You'll make it writing. I just know it."

Things happened fast after that, again almost as if we were following a script already written. Early in 1974, the magazine bosses killed *Top Operator*, the special *Farm Journal* publication I was by then assigned to. I was assured that my place in the company was not in jeopardy, but it was a golden excuse to quit if I could get severance pay. *Farm Journal* agreed to that. I think the editors knew I should be moving on anyway. I called Jerry Goldstein at *Organic Gardening*. He ran the day-to-day operation there, and I had gotten to know and like him. In fact he had already tried to hire me. I told him I was going home. Would he be interested in seeing what I would write on a continuing basis about going back to the land? He responded positively. Next, I called my brother-in-law Denny, a comrade from the seminary who had married Marilyn and was now a realtor. I asked him to start looking for a country place with acreage for us. I knew it would not be an easy task because the grain farmers in our fertile county were doing so well at the moment that they didn't want to sell anything. But Denny knew how to move mountains or at least make them come to him, and he soon found a spot and only two miles from the home place. My great aunt had walked into his office and said she had heard I was looking for land. She had twenty-two acres she would sell, with a woods and creek.

"Plenty of people have tried to buy that property for a building lot," Denny said, "but she wouldn't sell it, you, you, rotten lucky sonavabitchin' Davy Crockett boy."

Carol and I bundled up the kids and headed for Ohio in a spring snowstorm. We were as full of apprehension and excitement as any family heading west a century or two earlier.

At home we walked back through the property. Balboa could not have been as excited when he first sighted the Pacific. The acreage, which I had not walked on for twenty-five years, was everything that I remembered and more—amazingly like the "perfect" homestead that I had described in my book. Two acres along the road for gardens, then five acres of woodland, where we would put the house and barn, then a hill pasture of about seven acres descending to about five acres of rich creek-bottom land through which ran a never-failing stream. And because the land was hilly and mostly not the best corn and soybean ground, the price was a reasonable $700 an acre. As I walked, my pace quickened. A lightness came to my feet as well as to my spirit. Soon I was trotting, then running, leaving Carol and the kids behind. Magic was in the air. A woodcock flushed from the brush along the woods, and there on the ground was a sight seldom seen—a clutch of woodcock eggs, usually well camouflaged but now plainly visible because of the mantle of snow around it.

I had actually made it back home to stay. I was remembering now earlier days on this very land: hunting arrowheads, fishing with Cousin Bernard, setting traps and turtle lines with my father. I leaped the creek and, still running, climbed the hill beyond, the farthest reach of our new paradise. From there I could see a Wyeth painting and a Berry poem in every direction across the countryside. Beyond last year's stubbled cornfields to the east, beyond pastures and woodlots of my childhood haunts, the home-farm silos stood gaunt against the sky, the silos that I had helped build seventeen years ago with such naive faith in agribusiness. I could see Cousin Ade's place and Cousin Raymond's too, the lay of the land remarkably unchanged since the days of my childhood. It had been years since I stood out in open country like this with only a few distant farmhouses in view, nestled in silent peacefulness.

I had beaten the economic and religious rap that had kept me from this place. Like a bad dream, the various steps of my slow, stumbling journey to get back to where I belonged sped across my memory, took wing, and disappeared forever over the horizon of time. I was, as much as one could wish for in America of 1974, at age forty-three, free of people telling me how I had to live to "reach my full potential." I looked north, back over the twenty-two acres that would be our home. Suddenly, without thinking, I threw back my head and whooped in exultation. Carol, below me, watching, waved in understanding. I waved back. Even from a distance, I could see the smile on her face.

CHAPTER 6 / *Settling In*

More than anything else, the degree of satisfaction to be gained from a life rooted in home depends on the strength of one's conviction that there is nothing better down the road. Betterment comes from within a person, not from within geography. But I believe that had I not left home for awhile, I would not have been completely convinced of that. There would always have been a lingering question in my mind: Would life somewhere else have been more pleasant? Living in seven other places in five other states, and traipsing over much of the rest of the United States as a writer relieved me of that doubt. All places were about the same, with regard to people. There was no escaping human nature, no matter where Utopia might seem to exist.

Traveling and closely observing farming and gardening all over the United States had also convinced me that the fertile corn-belt soil in the eastern Midwest was as good as any place for garden farming, and better than most. Its only drawback was occasionally frigid weather, but that killed insect pests and made organic methods easier to follow than in the warmer South. American horticulturist Luther Burbank said that the person who really wanted to devote his life to gardening should move to California. That was understandable for him since he tried first in New England, where climate shortened the gardening year considerably. But California today was not his California at the turn of the

century. It had become a seething frenzy of unrelenting growth.
People with Burbank's instincts were moving away from there. But
the wide open spaces of the West were too dry to suit me; I was
thirsty the entire time I traveled in that glorious landscape, even
though it happened to rain most of that trip. Much of the North
was too cold for the farming and gardening I envisaged, though I
loved it there in many ways. The East was too crowded; the South
too hot.

In addition to weather considerations, the eastern cornbelt
where I had settled possessed some of the richest soils in the world.
I became convinced that it could support a diversity of plants and
animals equal to that of the rain forest. That capability lay hidden
from social and agricultural view only by tall corn's stranglehold
on the farmer's mind. Economics enforced a semi-monoculture of
corn, soybeans, and sometimes wheat on land where every temperate crop in the world could be grown successfully. Hardwood
forests thrived so well, even on upland soil, that had reforestation
of only the hilly land that was wasted to surplus corn taken place,
we would today have ample supplies for furniture and structural
wood, plus enough lesser-grade wood to give us a significant supply of heating fuel and methane. And the millions of dollars spent
to subsidize rich landowners for putting land into conservation
reserve programs would not have been necessary. Hops, ginseng,
hemp, canola, flax, rape, barley, spelt, and millet, as well as all the
commoner grains except rice, had been grown successfully here.
Every temperate fruit and vegetable would flourish here. Wild
animals would repopulate in abundance here, given a chance. Deer,
Canada geese, and wild turkeys were becoming pests where they
had not existed at all when I was young. Wolves and coyotes, also
unknown to my youth, were on the prowl. Slowly it became clear
to me that wildlife in fact was going to be not only my biggest joy
but biggest problem. The best answer to that problem seemed to
be to eat the excess. (Little did I realize then the stir such a viewpoint would generate in a society so far removed from natural reality.) I became convinced we could get all the meat we needed

from nature on our farm if we really wanted to. I reckoned our farm had a yield of about four groundhogs, three raccoons, six rabbits, and one-fourth of a deer per acre per year. The woodlot for sure produced a steady output of six squirrels per acre even with heavy hunting. A poor farm family I had known in Minnesota derived a good third of its meat from squirrels, rabbits, and occasionally a feast of red-winged blackbird breasts. We could do that too, if necessary, without at all hurting, and indeed helping, wildlife.

Farm ponds were immensely practical here and could supply unknown and unestimated quantities of fresh, unpolluted fish equal in taste to any the ocean has to offer. It was not long before we built one ourselves.

Botanically, we began from nearly the first day to increase the farm's diversity. We began moving in wildflowers once native to the locale: bluebells, Dutchman's britches, toadshade, hepatica, white trillium, shooting star, bloodroot, firepink, butterfly weed, yellow water lily, large-flowered bellwort, purple cress, and wild phlox, along with naturalized grape hyacinths, forget-me-nots, windflowers, several kinds of violets, snowdrops, and Siberian squill, which spread farther into the lawn every year where we did not mow before June. These flowers joined with a host of wildflowers already here: rue anemone, woods anemone, violets, jack-in-the-pulpit, wild hyacinth, wild geranium, wild bergamot, wild rose, Deptford pink, spring beauty, Quaker ladies, Canada lily, swamp milkweed, spiderwort, wild flag, wild aster, and others I did not know the names of. This project, coupled with introducing new tree species, was delightfully unending.

Hardly a day went by that I did not thank the gods for most of the world's tendency to ignore the cornbelt. The humdrum Midwest? That's what made it so precious. There was nothing much to tempt "economic development," except horrid animal factories, which at least had the effect of scaring away urban out-migration. There was nothing to attract the ecologically illiterate tourist to violate our privacy; nothing to charm the media into turning us into lies. No breathtaking views of either mountain or valley lured the vacationer, nor large body of water put our property taxes at the mercy of rich people's condos and second homes. No famous event of history had occurred here. No one nationally well known lived here. Our county appeared to urban America as a dull, plain landscape inhabited by dull, plain people, and we fervently hoped that we could keep that image alive. We were saved by an accident of geography, the only armor that could effectively fend off the cursed greed of "increase and multiply and dominate the earth." We lived in Flyover Land and prayed that it would stay that way.

We might have gone back to Carol's home in Kentucky, but it didn't exist anymore. It had been wiped out by houses and factories. People and traffic swarmed as hectically over that once lovely land as around Louisville and Lexington. The only acreage we could find there that we could afford was so steep that even a horse might fall off of it. (Once we traded one of our flatland ewe lambs to Wendell Berry for one of his rams. He claimed that until she got used to his hills, every time she lay down and fell asleep, she would forget where she was and roll downhill a couple of turns.)

○

The real success of going home anywhere, of making a place a home, is spousal generosity. During the years at *Farm Journal* we saved money that we might have spent easily enough. Carol could have insisted on a bigger house, but she made the little one we had cozy with love. She could have insisted on fancy clothes, but she made her own fancier than those in the upscale stores. She could have insisted on a bigger car, but appearances weren't that important to her either. She could have insisted on expensive private schools for the kids—we lived very close to one. But she was wise enough to know that upscale private schools were no guarantee of anything. We saved the money we had to have to go back home.

It took about five years to build our homestead into a bare-bones model of an ecological food-production system. First came a house, naturally enough. We lived in a rather dilapidated farm-house a few miles away while the new one was being built. We did not, however, build an ecologically smart house because we didn't know any better then. But at least the lower floor was built into the earth, split-level fashion, and so the family room and what would be my office were always easy and economical to heat or cool. We would eventually solve the heating problem upstairs with a wood-burning stove, while the big oaks outside cut down considerably on summer heat.

Strawberry and asparagus beds we started immediately, along with an orchard. Fencing began immediately around the perimeter of the farm. Always pressed for money, I found used woven wire fencing and posts, slashing the cost of one of the garden farm's most expensive outlays. I was in no hurry to get the crossfences complete, because I wasn't sure yet where to put them. The pasturelands, pitifully exploited by cash-grain farming, needed time to be brought into enough productivity to support livestock. Lime, chemical fertilizer, manure, and routine mowing almost magically regenerated the hillsides into a fair stand of volunteer clovers and native grasses in three years.

We built a scraggly looking chicken coop out of used lumber and a crude corn crib from sapling logs cut out of the woods. Since I was writing furiously all the while, the work went slowly. But that was probably for the better, because every day of experience brought more intelligence to the decisions of where to position buildings, how they ought to be designed for our particular needs, where to put the crossfencing in the pastures, and what grains and clovers grew better in our soil. We built the main barn in the third year, Mom and kids manning hammers and paintbrushes too. By this time I knew the best place for the barn: on the east side of the woods, where the winter winds don't hit, and on the highest rise in the more or less flat landscape so that rain water flowed away from the barn, not into it.

The barn, fencing, and pasture all were ready for livestock

about the same time, beginning with two heifer calves and two ewe lambs. That way they could all grow up together, and natural expansion would replace the expense of buying larger numbers of adult animals. It was plain to see that the animals and the pasture kept improving each other. What would it be like in twenty years? I wondered excitedly. The possibilities were open-ended, perhaps limitless. All I understood for sure was that this kind of agriculture could become many times more efficient per unit produced than agribusiness cash-grain farming and animal factories.

I became a sort of ecological choir director, orchestrating the many diverse kinds of biological and botanical life into a food system that could almost run itself. The challenge seemed to me as interesting as that which a scientist or artist faced. It called for not only expertise in several different areas, but the artistic instinct of sensing how all living things related to each other to the farmer's advantage. That meant I could never learn enough, that I would always be mostly ignorant because these relationships were so complex and numerous as to be beyond complete intellectual embrace.

I realized I was never doing just one thing. By starting pawpaw trees on the farm (which, by the way, I learned could become a nuisance weed-tree), I also brought in the lovely zebra swallowtail butterfly, which lives on pawpaw leaves exclusively. By making sure oaks and hickories continued in the woods, I assured the continuation of the haunting luna moth. When I spread manure on the fields, I was in one action producing several desired goals: getting healthful exercise, cleaning out the barn to keep the animals healthier, fertilizing the crops, avoiding harsh chemical fertilizers and the air pollution from their manufacturing and transportation, and increasing the amount of organic matter in the soil. A pasture that would support three ewes and their lambs per acre will also support at the same time one-third cow per acre with no difference to the supply of grass available. In building a farm pond, I was (1) constructing a reservoir of water that would slow down the rush of rain off the farm, ameliorating erosion, flooding, and ultimately drouth; (2) supplying the livestock with drinking water; (3) providing an outlet for field drainage tile; (4) increasing the diversity of wildlife; (5) producing fish, frog legs, and turtle meat for the table; and (6) providing recreation for the family, not to mention the ducks. Each of these activities related to the others in untold and unknown beneficial ways. It had to be a certainty that biological processes were zillions of times more efficient than industrial processes. The result was not only eminently scientific in terms of food production, but eminently beautiful as art.

Adding to the challenge, I thought of my work as a model for a new kind of commercial garden-farm of the future. If I could net a thousand dollars from sheep on eight acres, which I finally did, a likeminded operation on eighty acres should be able to net ten thousand, a considerable net income to go along with other products from that farm or as a part-time activity done in conjunction with an off-farm job.

I constantly asked myself, What is the most amount of *healthful* food, shelter, fuel, clothing, and recreation that a particular parcel of land could produce with the least amount of technological and physical energy? Would I be able to answer that in one lifetime?

With the basic outline of a self-subsisting farm in place, we turned to filling in the details, as a painter would do after the main outlines of color and form have been laid out on the canvas. Like the painter, we sometimes brushed out one detail in favor of another, or maybe sandpapered an image off the canvas entirely and put in a different one. I kept fine-tuning the crop rotation in my little fields, never reaching the perfection I sought, usually because a blast of unfavorable weather demanded unforeseen changes. I dropped wheat out completely because it ceased to fit into the most efficient rotation for a garden farm. (I could get enough from a neighbor for our flour, but if that were not possible, I would grow our bread wheat in the garden.) I stopped growing oats for grain but just for hay. Oats for grain were cheap; hay turned out to be the crop we were always short of and the one most expensive to buy. Wheat and oats for grain both came out of the rotation also because for larger amounts, they required a mechanical harvester of some kind. That meant more machinery expense, more fossil fuel use. I found I could satisfy my livestock's grain needs better with corn, a considerable amount of which I could harvest by hand. I also learned that when weather was too wet to make oat hay, I could just let it go to grain and the lambs would eat it just fine in the field and grow fat and sassy.

In the garden, I began experimenting with a different idea for me—mulch beds that required tilling only occasionally, sometimes not at all for several years. Mulch-bed gardening cut down on the size of a garden because there was no need to leave row space for a garden tiller or cultivator. That also reduced the amount of technological energy needed to manage the garden.

The canvas continued to transform as we erased the old henhouse when our son built a new one. I built a new corncrib and made firewood out of the old one. Eventually we added two machine sheds alongside the main barn. But I marked it progress only when space in these buildings began to be used more for animals and other biological products of the farm, and less to house machinery. For example, where the grain harvester once was sheltered, we would eventually store and dry lumber from our own woods.

The work settled into a routine in due time. After a few years I could look at the calendar and tell just about what I'd be doing during any given week through the coming year. First there were the daily chores. In winter, I went to the barn twice daily to feed the animals: hay and maybe a little corn to the cow and sheep; hay, corn, and table scraps to the two fattening pigs; corn and table scraps to the chickens; water for all. Except in thaw time when the pastures were too soft for animals to traverse, the livestock went to the pond or creek for water, or ate snow. My last daily "chore" was to gather the eggs.

In March, activity started to pick up with boiling off a little maple sap and building or repairing fences. Also on the frozen ground of March I broadcast grass and clover seedings, fertilizer, and lime. While broadcasting seed and fertilizer, I also hunted for Indian artifacts as I walked and listened to the cardinals sing. All the livestock went on pasture by April after the ground was solid enough so that their hooves did not pockmark the sod with little holes. Each year as the permanent pasture grew stronger, I could let the animals out earlier.

Around the first of April, we butchered the hogs and smoked bacon and hams. Lambing began about that time too, keeping us on the run day and night.

By the first of May, if not sooner, we were in the thick of planting the garden and the oats and corn in the fields. But there was always time to hunt morel mushrooms and do some birdwatching as the warblers passed through going north. By the end of May, haymaking began, not only in the regular hay fields, but on the pastures that had gotten ahead of the grazing animals. June was for more hay, garden work, and cultivating the field corn. July meant making oat hay and otherwise staying out of the heat. In August, with the water low in the pond, we could harvest some fish, and if the bullfrog population increased, some of them too.

In August, I began to cut green corn for the animals as grass diminished and kept moving the livestock from field to field to take advantage of every green blade during this most difficult season for the grazier. Some pastures might need to be mowed for weed control, but the sheep usually did a good job of that. Harvest from the garden—canning, freezing, and drying—was heaviest now. Now was also the time to butcher broilers.

In September, the rains usually came again, relieving the grass situation, although sometimes I had to feed a little stored hay. I cut a little more hay too in September, unless drouth weather compelled grazing the hayfield.

In October we finished corn harvest and turned the livestock in to clean up the stalks. In November woodcutting began and continued through winter on milder days. I also hauled the lambs to market in November.

In December I plowed the old clover sod for next year's corn after grazing it hard. Victory was being able to extend the grazing season to Christmas. I looked forward to a day when there would be grazing yet in January, and wondered, from what I was learning, if some grazing might not be possible on some days in all months. This was another intriguing challenge.

In this cycle of work I never became bored or weary since there was never too much to do at one time. Although most of this work went forward in solitude, I never felt alone. If I was in a field where the sheep were grazing, they would come over and observe, like so many judges. The cow would examine every one of my pockets, hoping for an ear of corn. In the spring, a pair of Canada geese at the pond ranted and raved at my arrival as if they owned the place and I was the trespasser. When I walked around the pond, the fish followed me, hoping for worms. Our cat usually tagged along, except in hot weather. Along the fence rows, the bluebirds, kingbirds, chickadees, and field sparrows would say hello. The red-headed woodpeckers darted from cornfield to woods, scolding my intrusion. The downy woodpeckers and nuthatches noted my passing with their gravelly little churr-churrs, and the tufted titmice actually got on my nerves with their incessant, plaintive singsong. As grainfields ripened in the neighborhood, indigo buntings would surely show up. Great looping buzzards soared above me at all times, hoping that I would drop dead and provide them with a meal.

The wildflowers were steadier companions. They couldn't run away. In every season they came, some thirty to forty species that I could name; many that I could not. Some flourished where sheep grazed, some disappeared. Where grazing had been ongoing for many years and then stopped, lovely wild hyacinths grew up, but only for a few years, and then they disappeared as the brush forerunners of woodland took over. I suppose they will wait in the ground, evidently for centuries, to come up again in that certain mysterious stage of botanical development between grazing (or burning) and woodland. No one could explain this to my satisfaction.

The ghostly ghost flower (Indian pipe) came up once in our woods and never again. What triggered its appearance? The Indians said this flower without chlorophyll grew where humans lay buried. Why not?

For a number of years my most entertaining companions in all this work and play were my children. I died my first death when they grew up and made their own way in the world. But then two grandsons and a granddaughter came along to follow me all over the farm. When they came, their parents did too. And of course there was always Carol.

Was life from now on always going to be blissful?

CHAPTER 7 / *Killdeer Woman*

I didn't know how many times we told her not to climb up into the haymow to throw down bales to her calves. But my mother wouldn't listen. She never listened to people telling her to take it easy. People had been telling her all her life not to carry heavy buckets of feed to the chickens when she was pregnant, not to hoe her garden when her back hurt, not to get up at 4 A.M. to help with the milking when her kidney infection flared up. She paid no attention. She was contemptuous of physical weakness—and mental weakness too. She never let her nine children stand around feeling sorry for themselves. "When you grow up and get yourself some real problems, you'll think you deserve the luxury of a nervous breakdown," she would tell us. And then she'd give us more work to do.

So there she went, all alone, up into the mow again, probably singing (she was always singing), and as old as she was, she could climb a barn ladder almost as spryly as a seventeen-year-old. But something happened this time. No one will ever know how, but somewhere along the edge of the mow, she lost her balance and fell. Fell and broke her neck. Broke her neck and died.

But it didn't happen all that fast. She was too tough. She lay in the manure, unable to move or cry out. Dad found her there with their dog licking her face. She whispered that Tillie's licking her face felt good.

I do not understand how Dad took the pain. I was not there when she fell, but I could not even think about her lying there without almost losing my mind. But Dad stood it. And my brother stood it. And eventually we all stood it. Because Mom had taught us that you can stand anything when you have to.

In the hospital, the doctors put a pin in her head and attached a weight to it so her neck would not move. She complained only that they took away her false teeth—which none of us children knew she had worn for twenty years. Her head had to be shaved and ugly as that seemed to make her, for the first time I could tell how very much she looked like her father.

He had never given up either. When he was eighty-four, he demolished his pickup truck and walked away unhurt. After that the family would not let him drive from his house in town to his beloved home farm. So he walked. He would become confused, walk the wrong way and get lost. They forbade him to leave the house. He'd sneak out. Finally they took his shoes away from him. That was the only way they could keep him off his land.

And so now, my mother. She lay in the hospital a week, refusing to give up. She was paralyzed from the waist down but wouldn't admit it.

"Look, Gene," she'd say. "See how I can move my hands. See how strong my grip is." And I'd have to put my finger into the palm of her hand and she would try to grasp it. She could not turn her head to see that her hand, which had held nine children growing up, which had gripped countless hoe handles and tractor steering wheels and horses' reins, which had pulled milk from who knows how many cows, could not now hold on to even my slack finger.

But she kept working at it, flexing her arms, all day, all night. We could tell when she was conscious that way. Her hands would clench, open, clench, open. Even when she had no strength to talk, the fingers kept up the fight.

Finally she announced to all of us that she had given herself a goal. By the time Rosy, one of my sisters, had her baby in the spring, she'd be able to sit in a wheelchair and hold it in her arms, she declared. That's what she told us. And kept repeating. It was the very last thing she said to me.

But that was not the end of the story. Old farmers, like old soldiers, never die. They stamp a piece of land with an indomitable spirit that lives forever. This is how I know.

There were long gray days after that burial, days not fond to recall, when about the only thing that kept me sane were those words of hers which had kept us going before: "When you get yourself some real problems, you'll think you deserve the luxury of a nervous breakdown." I was traveling again at the time to make some money. Traveling by itself was extremely depressing to me anyway. Always in earlier years, I could lift the telephone in Chicago or Omaha or Saint Louis or wherever, call home, and she would always answer. So now I tried again to call down those long, lonesome wires of the homeless. But no one would answer. Dad was there, but he was always someplace working. Sisters were there, but they were always away. No one would answer. That is how I finally came to accept that Mom was dead. She did not answer the phone at home anymore.

A day came when I could go back to the cemetery. It was early spring, with only a little greening to it. I walked to the grave, prepared to have the sorrow all plowed up again. I was thinking about how stupid cemeteries were, the irrational symbolism of granite and plastic flowers and live people standing over bones becoming earth again. And maybe that feeling of irrationality prepared me for what I found on Mom's grave, because what I found bore not the scrutiny of logic. I found magic.

A bird, a killdeer, was sitting on a nest of eggs, on top of Mom's grave. The bird fluttered away at my approach, screaming in defense of her brood, pretending that she was hurt, trying to lure the intruder away from the life it was her life's work to protect.

Mom always loved killdeers—she liked to call her farm Killdeer Place. I had to smile. Ignoring the tombstone, I stooped to examine the eggs. Infuriated, the killdeer charged at me. She held up, an arm's length away, seeming to stamp her foot in the very way Mom used to do when she was angry. My sudden laugh rang out over the quiet cemetery. My children, who were with me, did not understand. They saw a bird and three eggs in the grass. I saw the spirit of my mother, screaming in defense of creation, turning even her grave into a green cradle of life.

CHAPTER *8 /* *The Blizzard*

When we came home, my first goal was to establish a beachhead of security against the man-made disaster of severe economic depression which I thought was imminent. While I was erroneously watching that horizon, I neglected to get ready for natural disasters as thoroughly as I should have. We were putting our independent food-production system in place as fast as we could, but there were little immediate details that I did not attend to. I thought we were safe enough. In an emergency, I could get water from the creek or from the buried rain barrels at the barn. If the electricity failed, I had gone to the expense of putting two fireplaces in the house for emergency heat. I thought we were prepared for anything, like good Boy Scouts.

When disaster struck, the fireplaces actually did keep us more or less alive without electricity, but I learned that unless you have a great pile of wood to waste and nothing else to do, a fireplace is not worth one-third the heat and cooking value of even a small, cheap wood-burning stove, let alone a good one. This was especially true when the wood I planned to burn was buried deep under the snow somewhere out in a howling blizzard several hundred feet from the house.

It started innocently enough, on the evening of January 24, 1978. Warm, for January, and a sleety mix of rain and snow out of the northeast. Beware of winter storms that start out in the northeast. Of the three weather reports I checked daily, only one showed any concern about the warm front pushing strongly from the south and a wild cold front rampaging along from the west. Even that report did not warn us of real impending danger until warning was too late. The two fronts collided right over Ohio and unleashed a blitzkrieg of snow never equaled here before or since.

First rain poured down and lightning flashed. Sometime after midnight the wind began to moan with a deep, forlorn sound unlike anything I'd ever heard, the kind of sound I imagine a herd of dinosaur mothers would make giving birth in unison. By morning the moan had turned into a roar, and all that could be seen out the windows was a blur of white on off-white, moving horizontally. When I stepped outside on my way to the barn, the raging wind tore my breath away. Breathing required concentration, as if there were not quite enough oxygen in the air. The snow was already a couple of feet deep, and walking was impossible. I could only wallow and flounder as I fought my way through the woods to the barn. Were it not for the familiar trees to show the way, I would have become lost like farmers I'd read about in North Dakota, who started for the barn in bad blizzards and froze to death wandering around in the white wrath. The wind by now had veered around to the southwest, so along the east side of the woods where the barn stood, the wind chill factor was not fatal, although even here, breathing was difficult.

I went first to the pig pen, since it was the flimsiest of the buildings, hardly more than a roof over a gated pen. The little shed was completely full of snow. My God, what had happened to the pig? Suddenly a black snout erupted, then a pig head, looking out at me quizzically, grunting, "What's for breakfast," as if nothing extraordinary were taking place. I laughed, though hardly in the mood for it. That pig in its snowdrift was as snug as a cat on the hearth.

I was astonished how the fine, hard-driven snow penetrated cracks as easily as water would have. The hay in the mows was covered with snow. Much of the pen space below was piled with snow drifts, some of them in exquisitely wind-sculptured shapes. The sheep and cattle did not seem particularly upset and only stared expectantly at me, waiting for hay as usual. I uncovered enough hay to throw down into their mangers. They had been eating snow and showed no interest in water. In the chicken coop, the hens sat on their roost in a huddled row like drunks humped along a ghetto store front. They showed no interest in eating. Two smart old biddies had climbed into the nestboxes to stay snug. I thought about putting the chickens over in the main barn with the livestock. In Minnesota, on below zero nights, I had seen hens roost on top of cows.

In the evergreen tree where the sparrows roosted, the little birds sat frozen stiff, occasionally dropping to the ground like ripe pine cones. The terribly heavy rain had soaked into their feathers, and the drastic quick-freeze that had followed killed them. A screech owl flapped nervously around the hay mow, having been shanghaied by the wind and sleet in the night. It had found shelter in the barn, I thought, only by accident and that's what saved its life. After the storm I would find red-headed woodpeckers frozen to death in fencepost holes, and blue jays and cardinals in fence corners. Our entire population of quail was wiped out.

By now the cold was getting to me—it was ten below and still dropping. The windchill factor had to be breaking records. Floundering back to the house, I almost panicked. I wasn't sure I was going to make it. I had to stop and catch my breath after every two or three slipping, sliding steps. Once I burrowed down in a drift to rest and was amazed at how comfortable I felt there, insulated from the driving wind. I was reminded of the old saying "No weather is ill, when the wind is still." I wondered how long I could survive there if I had to. But I was within sight of the house now, a grey blur through the driving snow, so I fought my way on. Crossing the yard where there was no protection from the wind, I was nearly swept away and had to crawl to make it to the door. At least here the snow was only about a foot deep.

Carol was waiting anxiously. "I don't believe I like Mother

Nature and the great outdoors after all," I said. I wanted to confess that I was scared, but thought better of it. The kids were enjoying the crisis. No school.

We were snug and tight in a new house that had been ultra-insulated for electric heat, and so we faced the storm more as an adventure than a danger. I wondered what the people living in mobile homes down the road were doing.

Then the electricity went off. The full meaning of the power outage did not at first strike us. We'd more or less enjoyed outages before. But none of them had ever occurred when the temperature was below zero. Our heating system was "total electric," tah dah. Everything in the house depended on electricity except the fireplaces. Okay. No big deal. That would be kind of fun.

That's when I realized that the wood was all out in ricks in the woodlot, several hundred feet from the house. I had been bringing it into the garage only on an as-needed basis. That several hundred feet became more like half a mile in the raging storm. Moreover, once I battled my way out there, I could not find the woodpiles! The deep snow obliterated all landmarks except for the trees themselves, which now looked all the same. It was like being in a boat on a pond, looking for a pocketknife that had dropped overboard. I groveled to the barn and fetched a steel fencepost to use as a probe. I groveled back and started jabbing down in the approximate area of a wood rick, astonished that the snow was six feet deep. Two feet to the top of a rick if I could locate the damn thing. I probed. I panted. I cussed enough to melt a little snow. Finally, shortly before frostbite set in (or shortly after, I'm not sure, because ever since, my fingers ache painfully when I'm out in severe cold), I found one of the ricks. All right! There was enough wood in it, I knew, to last for twenty-four hours, even for a greedy fireplace. Surely the electricity would be back on by then. I started to question my sanity for moving "back to the land," but then I remembered. At least we did have wood and a place to burn it. What were others doing, without any survival recourses?

I struggled all morning getting wood to the house, using the kids' toboggan to drag a few chunks at a time. With the fire roaring in the lower fireplace, sending a draft of warm air up the stairs to the kitchen, we breathed easier. No matter what, we would not have to evacuate. Carol, resourceful as ever, had made a huge pot of stew to hang over the fire, into which she had put everything that might have spoiled in the dead refrigerator. We could live on stew for a week if we had to.

It was obvious that keeping both fireplaces going was not prudent, considering the difficulty of getting wood to the house and the inefficiency of the fireplaces. We concentrated our efforts on the big fireplace in the downstairs family room from which the heat would rise up through the house, gaining a little more heat efficiency than the fireplace on the main floor. It was comparatively easy to keep the lower floor warm since, being of split-level design, it was half-buried in the ground. It was also almost totally buried by snow. We drained the water pipes to keep them from freezing upstairs. "We'll melt snow for water," I said, matter-of-factly.

Have you ever tried to melt snow in a pot over a fireplace? Brewing a bucket of beer would be a lot faster.

The telephones never went out, and we had the car radio to keep us informed of what was going on elsewhere. We were, in fact, in better shape than most people. Neighbors with snowmobiles and ways to keep their homes at least partially warm were rescuing those who did not. One family had a wood stove in their garage workshop, and survived there along with the people from next door. Others just holed up in bathrooms, sitting in the tub and draping blankets around them, gaining a bit of heat and light from tin cans full of burning candles. We took in the two families near us who were without heat of any kind. In our cozy lower-level family room, we ate stew and drank beer and played cards till midnight, all in a festive spirit. I warned everyone that the toilet did not flush, and put a bucket in the bathroom to use for a chamber pot. But some guests used the toilet anyway, out of sheer habit, I guess, or totally befuddled at the notion of being without a flush toilet. How fragile our society is.

Too dull to realize it myself, I learned from the radio that I could drain maybe thirty gallons of water out of the water heater. I used some of it to flush the toilet. I absolutely forbade its usage after that. "Use the bucket, brave the storm, go to the barn like I did, or back to your own house," I said.

I never did learn to quit flicking the light switch every time I went into a dark room.

That night, everyone finally fell asleep except me. The whole floor was littered with bodies in blankets and sleeping bags. I stayed awake in a stuffed chair, feeding the fire. The only sound was the snapping of the wood, that unearthly, deep, moaning roar of wind outside, and some of the most godawful snoring that I have ever heard.

By the second night there was nothing party-like about the situation. We were tired of eating stew, tired of sleeping on floors if at all, tired of not being able to take a bath, tired of going up to the barn to defecate, tired of trying to melt snow, and tired of being snowbound in one room with neighbors. What would we do in this country if we had to experience the ravages of war? What kept everyone fairly cheerful was the belief that the electricity would soon be restored. If I'd known I had two more days to go, I might have climbed in the car and driven south until I ran into warm sunshine. But of course the roads were impassable.

By the afternoon of the second day the wind calmed a little, the sun peeked out a little, and though the coming night would sink to twenty-eight below, things seemed a little brighter without the fierce gale. The snowplow finally got one lane open on the road, and farmers on snowmobiles and huge tractors were bringing food and aid wherever needed. I walked down the cleared path on the road to my elderly neighbors, thinking they might need some help with something. I almost laughed when I got into their house. Their woodburning furnace, their usual method of heating, was keeping the whole house toasty warm, life as usual. They had a cookstove too and were enjoying a bounteous supper. They had emptied the contents of their freezer into a snowdrift on the porch. They were better off than anyone, which is to say, the storm made no difference to their usual lifestyle. As they told me, smiling, they had often been ridiculed for being old-fashioned and heating with wood. "There are those around here who think only poor folk cut and burn wood," the farmer said with a great deal of satisfaction. Even the doves and starlings and sparrows of their barnyard were not in jeopardy. They were clustered around the top of the chimney, basking in the warm air arising from it. When I came back home, I noticed with satisfaction that a few birds were enjoying our chimney too.

The morning of the third day I cut down the dead hickory tree close to the house and split it up for wood, which was easier than trying to dig more snow-coated wood from the rick farther away. We transferred freezer food to snowdrifts like our neighbors had done. I shoveled snow out of the barn and chicken coop and put down lots of fresh dry straw, so the animals might have considered themselves better off than usual. For sure, the deep snow covering almost everything to rooflines was acting as excellent insulation. The sheep still seemed content with snow for water, but I finally got the cover off the underground rain barrels to water the two cows and chickens and pig. Because of the deep snow, the water in the barrels had only a thin covering of ice despite the severe cold.

The evening of the third day, neighbors a mile away, on a different utility line, had their electricity restored. Carol and the kids went over to my sister's for a hot meal, a bath, and a warm environment. For our place, there was one more day of weak fireplace heat and using a plastic bucket for a chamber pot, and then we had electricity too. Since then I've never complained very loudly about hydroelectric dams, nuclear power plants, or coal-burning generators.

But all our discomfort and worry could easily have been avoided with a good, wood-burning parlor stove and a way to get water out of the ground by hand. Before winter came again, I had a big, black, motherly, cast iron Defiant stove in the living room, closing off the fireplace opening forever. The Defiant was capable of heating the main floor and the upstairs comfortably and easily. If I used the fireplace downstairs in conjunction with the stove, we could keep the house at seventy-eight degrees no matter how cold it got outside. Cooking on the stove was not difficult; it just took a little getting used to.

Since then we have endured other winter power-outages (though none as long) with ease, even with peace, because there is a sort of wonderful silence that embraces a house without electricity.

With a stove going full blaze, it is almost practical to melt snow in a pot on it too, solving the water problem. Nor is it too difficult, with a copper boiler on the stove, to heat water enough for a bath in an emergency.

For water without electricity, a cistern with a hand pump on it would be the better solution—like the one we relied on all the time when I was a child—before we had electricity. Or I could spend a lot of money on a windmill and hand pump combination for a well, or just install a hand pump down the well casing for about $300. Eventually I learned about a simple way to rig up a hand pump for less than fifty dollars by using the lowly foot valve, available through hardware stores, attached to the bottom of a length of PVC pipe long enough to reach down the well casing to a foot or two below water level. By "pumping" the pipe up and down vigorously with your hands, the foot valve will lift water to the surface. A weep hole in the pipe, just above the foot valve, will make sure that water drains back out of the pipe and doesn't freeze. You can attach a garden hose to the top of the pipe to convey the water out into a container. Survivalists believe that this bit of simple information could save lives someday, and they may be right.

Having endured the blizzard of '78, but barely, I am in awe of Amish houses now. We visit one frequently. A big parlor stove dominates their living room too. Water flows by gravity, underground from a cistern on a hill above the house. A windmill pumps water into the cistern on windy days. The kitchen stove is gas-powered, and so are the refrigerator and water heater. Out in the barn is a diesel generator that supplies electricity to the milk tank and the milking machines. "Blizzard of '78?" my Amish friend repeats with a pixie grin, pretending he can't remember. "Was it really any worse than any other winter?"

CHAPTER 9 / *Lessons "The Crick" Taught Me*

Our family called the stream that ran through our land "The Crick" ever since my parents brought me to live beside it in 1934. On the old maps, it was designated as Warpole Run, no doubt after the Wyandot Indian chief War Pole, who lived in these parts. As creeks go, The Crick was quite small, much smaller than Tymochtee Creek, into which it flowed a few miles west of our place. At normal water level, it was too wide through our farm to jump over except where little clumps of islands split the stream into narrower rivulets or where light-footed boys could, with a running start, leap from one of the six-vertical-foot banks at the outside curve of a meander to a lower bank on the opposite side. Upstream two miles, closer to its origins, where The Crick ran through Old Home, jumping it was a little easier. The number of times that I had tried and failed was incalculable. But no amount of negative experience ever kept me from trying again. The Crick told me that "he who loveth danger shall perish in it," but I never learned. Having gained the other side of the creek by perilous jumping, I felt compelled to jump back again, proceeding downstream or upstream, back and forth until, sure enough, I landed in the stream. That meant hurrying home with a boot or shoe full of water to tell Mom that I had a "leaky boot," as if somehow it were the boot's fault that I had once more ignored The Crick's warnings and been lured into its seductive current. Now when I jumped and missed, I made the excuse that I was getting old.

No toy when I was a child nor substitute for a toy as a man, not even my beloved ball diamond, entertained me nearly as much or as long as The Crick. As children, my siblings and I spent most of our free time playing alongside it, never tiring of its attractions. Though it was too shallow, except in flood time, for serious swimming, we waded whenever Mom would allow us, and built rock dams to deepen and widen the stream, which invariably meant getting soaked.

Marilyn, my sister, recently refined a variation on dam-building. She told her grandchildren that she had discovered a "singing place" along the creek, where the water sang songs. Off she trooped with two little grandsons, mystified and full of expectation, only to find that the rapids behind Kerr's Woods, to which Grandmaw had referred, had been more or less swept away in the last flood flow. The children were crestfallen.

"Tell you what," said Grandmaw. "We'll just make a new singing place."

And with that she took off her boots and socks, rolled up her sleeves and jeans, and began carrying rocks from the banks and creek bed, plopping them into the fast current where the water narrowed. Soon she had created little rapids and a watery chatter of splashing, gurgling sounds.

"Now there," she said. "You can hear the music begin. All we need are more rocks to get a whole symphony going. A few violins here, a trombone and flute over there, and maybe a pie-ano yonder."

The two boys grasped the possibilities immediately. They began to gather rocks and place them in the creek bed with an even more studied gravity than Grandmaw, as if they were professional creek music-makers.

"Okay, Grandmaw, listen close," the eight-year-old commanded. "Which sound do you like better? With this green rock right here and the grey one in back of it?" He paused for her to listen. "Or if I turn them around like this?"

All three listened intently. "Move the green one a little to the left, I believe," Grandmaw answered after due consideration. "Gives the music a little more bounce and babble. Otherwise that grey rock sounds too churchy for brook song."

The other little boy smiled broadly, catching on fast, as children are so good at doing with make-believe. He rolled a good-sized boulder into the water, then soberly cocked his ear up next to it. "It doesn't sound gurgly enough in this place," he said, displaying great erudition. He moved the rock closer to the others. "There, that's a real crick gurgle."

An hour of watery orchestration slipped by as fast as the water tumbling over the rocks, and the three, blissfully wet and muddy, sank into happy exhaustion on the bank to listen to their symphonic handiwork.

"I can hear it better with my eyes closed," said the younger of the boys. "I think it's singing 'Yankee Doodle Dandy'."

Silence. Then the older boy said. "I really don't think The Crick's singing at all. Just humming."

When the weather was too cold for wading, Carol and I walked the shoreline or the ice, or skated it (downstream, terrific speeds were possible) usually in company with children and grandchildren. In fall and spring we still fished, or hunted for arrowheads and "pretty rocks," raced wooden boats, or simply hiked along, always with the half-desired and exciting fear that we might fall in or slip and, darn, get another leaky boot.

I was familiar with The Crick from its beginnings northwest of Harpster to its end, where it flowed into Tymochtee Creek, a distance of maybe seven miles counting meanders. It connected Old Home with New Home, and so I saw it as a sort of umbilical cord. The two-mile stretch that flowed from Old Home to New Home I knew as intimately as the lines on the palms of my hands—every bend, every deep hole, every tributary, every septic tank draining into it. Some of the septic tanks were functioning properly and some were merely straight exhaust pipes from human assholes to the creek. But I dared not criticize others too much because in the years when we milked a hundred cows, I followed the practice of letting runoff from a barnyard full of manure flow unhindered into the creek. We just didn't know any better then, and the ignorance continued to this day.

Certain stretches of The Crick I saw every day, others every week or month, and a few parts perhaps only once a year. Those parts that I had not visited for a year I anticipated returning to as keenly as I imagined other people looked forward to returning to a wintering spot in Florida. What I returned to every day or every week I anticipated only a little less than that.

I couldn't tell you why I was drawn to this little stream or to flowing water in general. Steven Semken, in his lovely *River Tips and Tree Trunks* devoted a whole book to not explaining the mysterious attraction of rivers. The Grand in Michigan, in which I nearly drowned twice, and the Minnesota in Minnesota, which came close to killing me only once, were certainly grander than The Crick, but my knowledge of this little stream became with time so intimate and detailed that in it I could experience larger rivers, and do so a little more safely. Actually The Crick in floodtime became a raging torrent as dangerous in its undertows as any river, a fact I understood only gradually. Another lesson learned.

Perhaps my fascination with such a little, humdrum stream stemmed from the fact that I could encompass it all in my head and in my experience, a spatial whole of less than seven miles. I could also see it as a microcosm. I imagined the Niagara Falls in The Crick's water tumbling over a rock dam I threw across the creek. Minnows leaping up over the little dam provided as much drama as salmon leaping upstream on the Yukon. If I lay on my belly on the ice just above an open rapids, I could see up under the ice a marvelous array of crystalline formations hanging from the "ceiling" of the ice like miniature stalactites. If I took a photograph of these little icy encrustations when the sun was shining down through the ice, and gave no hint in the picture of the true size of these formations, the scene appeared to be some sculptured fantasia as awe inspiring as anything in the vast frozen worlds of Alaska or Greenland. Some nights in the fall, when rain had not fallen for a considerable time and the only water in The Crick was from the springs that fed it, I could shine a flashlight into the deeper holes, see thousands of minnows milling around, and pretend I was snorkeling along a coral reef.

The Crick, like an unrepentant drunk, meandered part of the time and tried to go straight the other. But straightness in a stream was a temporary and unnatural condition, and realizing that properly was another precious lesson learned. The two straightest parts of The Crick were man-made, one by my father, cutting off a looping bend that was threatening to meander into one of his fields, and one by my great-grandfather, cutting off another loop to gain a little more farmland. In the latter case, the straight ditch was already beginning to wiggle again. The start of a new wiggle was almost imperceptible. A tree trunk growing up on the bank or an exposed rock would create a slight obstruction to the water, and when the current at floodtime hit the obstruction, it bounced, almost as faithfully as a rubber ball, although invisibly, toward the opposite bank, causing the water to gouge into that bank ever so slightly. Gradually, with repeated gouging, a curve sprouted and the more pronounced the bend became the "faster" it continued to bend. After hundreds of years, the current would cut through the ever-narrowing stem of the bend until the latter was cut off completely into an oxbow. Although meander-growth was measured by decades and centuries, I could see it happening every day, if I looked closely enough. The realization was awesome. Water moved downstream, certainly, but The Crick itself moved from side to side like a squirming snake in very slow motion. That slow motion taught a great lesson in patience. Its sinuous bending held water from rapid descent to floodplains, lessening the threat of floods, but the meanders themselves meandered only so far and then were cut off, The Crick keeping itself within acceptable borders.

The best way to examine a creek was to walk in it, upstream. Then things like mussel shells or Indian artifacts were easy to see because the mud my footsteps stirred up floated away behind me in the current, while ahead the water remained clear. But whether I could see into the water depended on the position of the sun at any given time. Sometimes I had to walk on one of the other banks to gain the proper angle of light. If my intent was to see live animals in or on the water, I had to sit patiently on the bank or on a log over the water. The fish were extremely wary and clever, probably because they had so little water in which to flee predators. Casual passers-by might walk along a creek for years and not be aware of what the overhanging banks, water-soaked logs, or submerged rocks were hiding. One year some young pike migrated upstream from the Tymochtee during the spring floods and became trapped in the widest place of The Crick, next to the Indian Mound. The pike grew to eighteen inches long. My son caught a couple of them but it took great stealth. Drawing near to the Indian Mound, we would crawl on hands and knees till we were broadside of the water. Then, without standing up, he would cast a daredevil lure into the water and reel the line toward him, still on his hands and knees. When one of the pike launched out from its hiding place along the bank, waves rippled as if a whale were coursing the shallow stream. The secret to the fishes' survival was, of course, that there are occasional deep holes, some three feet deep, along the course of the stream. Although nothing like when I was a boy, a surprising number of small fish could be seined from these deeper holes. But that too took a certain skill, as the fish could easily slip around the seine into overhanging roots and grasses along the bank.

Even within the two miles of creek from our farm back up to Old Home there were striking ecological differences. About halfway between the two segments, springs bubbled up in the bed of the creek, keeping our part from drying up in drouth weather. At one time, there was a large spring on the creek bank at this point. Above this location, The Crick regularly went dry in August, starting to do so drastically when I was a child. I remember how the first time the deep holes dried up on Old Home, I carried buckets of sunfish, chubs, and bullheads to the horse trough in our barnyard, hoping to save them. Other chubs and suckers and smaller dace and minnows would return from downstream in spring floods, but seldom after that did I see bluegills, bullheads, and grass pike in the upper reaches of the creek. Wes Smith, who lived next to our farm and roamed The Crick when he was a boy, was ninety when I talked to him about it in the 1970s. In his early days (1890 to 1900), he said quite large bass and catfish could be caught routinely in The Crick and that from wading in it often, he reckoned the water averaged waist deep, considerably more than now. Cousin Ade, who would be approaching ninety-five if still alive, said that the Deep Hole, next to his sawmill above the springs, regularly produced two- and three-pound fish. So there had been a gradual decline in the aquacultural life and vitality of The Crick. Muskrats had become scarcer too, and so mink, which feed on them, become rarer too or turned to other prey. One year a mink killed all our hens.

Examining old maps, I was surprised to find that the locations of springs were marked, including the one mentioned above. Were these markings accurate? On the map, one spring stood either on or near our property line. Questioning Cousin Al, whose land borders ours, I learned that indeed there had been a notable spring at the edge of his woods, just across our common fenceline. A very well-defined depression, where water used to stand continuously, he said, and where there was still a little pool in springtime, marked the location. Talking to another cousin, Raymond, he off-handedly mentioned another big spring, well known in his youth. He told me where it had been, and sure enough, the 1889 map showed a spring at that location. A fourth spring, on a tributary of The Crick, given good display on the old map, I found still existed in a much diminished form, merely oozing up in the streambed to make a bit of a pool in dry weather when this tributary was otherwise without water.

The predominance of those springs, diminished if not gone entirely now, made a significant statement about environmental degradation. The degradation of our creek water was not just from runoff silt and chemical pollution directly, but from disappearing springs that once poured ample supplies of clean water into the stream year-round. Tile drainage of farmland, along with intensive cultivation, were the main destroyers of these springs, not environmental pollution. They removed rainwater before it could seep down to groundwater and then well back up as springs. Without the springs, the little creeks had only rain runoff to keep the current moving. Not only would the stream dry up regularly during droughty weather, but the water would be of low quality when it was present, full of silt from erosion as well as chemicals, and more prone to oxygen shortages in hot weather. If the springs still ran, the content of polluting materials in the stream would be less of the whole and so less devastating. One year, a massive fish-kill occurred on The Crick. I was convinced someone dumped toxic chemicals into it, but the game warden ruled that the cause was "oxygen starvation" from low-quality water.

The section of The Crick through our farm demonstrated the beneficial effects of the ever-flowing springs. The water here ran year-round, and while the abundance of fish seemed to me to be diminishing over the last twenty-two years, there was still much more aquatic life here than above the springs. Unlike the upper stretches, we even had mussels, etching their initials in the mud of the creek bottom as they inched their way along. These mussels (we called them clams) had to be extraordinarily tough to have survived so many years of pesticides, muddy runoff, high waters, drouth, raccoons, and great blue herons. Every year when the spring floods subsided and the weather warmed up, I feared that they would be gone. But so far, so good. Or rather, so far, not too bad.

This "ever-running stream" also assured us of great blue herons, little green herons, even kingfishers. Wild ducks of various kinds still came and went. Snapping turtles remained in diminished numbers, but painted turtles disappeared. Crayfish remained but not nearly as numerous as in my childhood days when it was easy to seine a bucket full of them.

When I dumped a big pile of rocks in the water to form a sort of rapids, a family of black rat snakes took up abode, delighting in the rocks to hide under and from which to dart out to grab minnows. They loved crawling up on the horizontal boards of the floodgate across the water to sun themselves. But they eventually disappeared.

I once spotted a solitary sandpiper bobbing and wading the creek, a rare sighting here, but so far the most unusual creature was a smallish brown thing diving into the water and streaking along underwater at a speed my eyes could barely follow. My best guesses were a Virginia rail, which can swim underwater, or a star-nosed mole, but my eyes have not been quick enough to identify the creature for sure.

The other unusual survivor found in our part of The Crick and not upstream, or indeed in any other stream around, was the yellow pond lily. It had grown in a stretch near the Indian Mound all my life despite regular rampaging floodwaters. Being a romantic, and because water lilies were used by the Indians for both food (root and seeds) and for medicinal purposes, I liked to think the Adena and Hopewell moundbuilders started the pond lilies there, just as I thought these earliest farmers of my land nurtured the pawpaw tree, which was botanically a tropical fruit that was not supposed to grow in the north but did. Sheep indirectly nurtured the pond lilies for the past hundred years by keeping down the brush and trees along the banks. Now that sheep no longer grazed this part of The Crick, brushy vegetation was growing out over the water and the lack of full sun seemed to be slowly diminishing the lilies. Sometimes a new lily from a piece of dislodged root or a seed would sprout and grow in my section, where sheep still grazed away the brush. But the plants never established themselves on our property as they had for so long only a couple hundred feet away. Another mystery.

Sheep made the whole valley of The Crick a comely place until twenty years ago. From here to Old Home and downstream to the Tymochtee, the creekside bottoms and shouldering hills were grass pastures, kept like a savanna by sheep ever since R. N. Taylor, starting on the prairies between the Tymochtee and the Sandusky in the early 1800s, converted this land to sheep ranching. These comely pastures made Andrew Wyeth paintings all along my childhood domain, which is probably why I love his work so much. The woodlots along the way were park-like, the trees widely dispersed over a sward of grass. This was not good for the woodlots exactly because the sheep ate all the seedling trees, but it was beautiful savanna to look at and wonderful to walk through and play in. I was always somewhat amused at city parks and college campuses and institutional lawns which were kept tidy and neat at great expense and much gagging of the air with mower-motor fumes and chemicals. Along The Crick, sheep and a few savvy shepherd-farmers kept hundreds of acres as a park and made money doing so.

But now, without sheep, these little valleys and open woodlots were growing back toward primeval forest. The advance of brush and trees was fascinating to watch. The German in me itched to mow all that trashy brush down and return the sheep, to keep the place looking orderly like a park or golf course. But the Irish in me delighted in seeing the forest return. In the end, I compromised: I kept sheep on one side of the creek most of the time and allowed the other to grow more wild. Perhaps one day more springs would start flowing again and some future moundbuilder would catch three-pound bass in The Crick again.

The most precious lesson The Crick taught me was the joy of cooperating with nature instead of forever beating my head against the wall of biological logic. Up at Old Home, The Crick was too close to its sources to ever flood out of its banks to any destructive degree, but on our land just two miles or so downstream, late-winter flooding, and even summer downpours, could turn the gentle stream into a violent river and then into a vast lake covering all the bottomland. The first time this happened I watched slack-jawed and horrified as the water rose over the top of my six-inch corn and ruined it. No wonder the oldtimers never farmed the rich bottoms next to the stream. For about five years, The Crick and I kept arguing about who owned those bottoms. Eventually The Crick won, but how willful I could be in my own agenda. After I watched floods rise in the wheat until only the heads were above water; after I watched a beautiful stand of oats knocked flat; after I watched windrowed hay float away and pile up against the fence in an almost indestructible mess, wisdom finally overcame stubbornness. I turned this land into permanent pasture. A wonderful thing then happened, as if nature were rewarding me for finally getting the point. Because this was the richest soil on the place (the reason I so persistently wanted to crop it) the grass grew abundantly, giving me better return in grazing than I could possibly have gotten from grain. And without any effort on my part. What's more, a kind of wild bluegrass or red top (I can't tell which, but an expert said bluegrass) spread into this field from the permanent pasture on the creek bank that was much more of a miracle plant than all those weird foreign forages that grassland-farming magazines were advertising so hard and which I had tried. This grass stayed green until Christmas. Then in the dead of winter, snow, ice, or water from flooding stood on this land and often protected this miraculous grass from freezing temperatures. At the first touch of thaw in late February, the grass began to green up and grow a little. It provided a little grazing for the sheep in March, saving me precious hay.

Why was it so hard for us humans to listen to our land, to listen to the songs of our creeks, the blood veins of the land?

A major joy of returning home was once again having access to good, cold, clean, clear well water. One of the little fictions that science tried to foist on us was that water was composed of two parts hydrogen and one part oxygen. Any country schoolchild knew better than that, or did before the Pepsi generation came along. Every well, cistern, and water tower had its own unique water; hydrogen and oxygen had little to do with it. Connoisseurs who liked their water dry, for example, could sip (or puff) on "lime water" as it came out of wells in the northern part of our county. Lime water was about fourteen parts limestone, never mind the hydrogen and oxygen. An emptied glass dried immediately, leaving a whitish film on the surface. I wondered what it did to the stomach lining. The more you drank, my grandfather said of his well water, the thirstier you got. Three quarts in less than an hour and you were in grave danger of dehydration.

Sulfur water was better known than lime water because it was so hard to forget. It possessed the buoyant fragrance of rotten eggs due to a natural infusion of hydrogen sulfide. It was good, Cousin Ade used to say, "for the loosening of the bowels." Those unaccustomed to its delights found out that traveling the highways and byways of our rural countryside could be as hazardous as traveling in Mexico—Tecumseh's Revenge instead of Montezuma's. But aficionados of water insisted that just as a first-rate martini needs a dash of vermouth, so a good water needed a drop or two of hydrogen sulfide.

Some artesian water was so hard it almost clanked when it dripped. Though referred to as "iron water" in these regions, it owed its hardness as much to magnesium and calcium. Allowed unsoftened into the plumbing, iron water was capable of forming stalactites on a dripping faucet in less than a year. Gourmets who mixed their own waters liked to start with iron water, add a jigger of lime water, a squirt of sulfur water and finally about 80 ppm of sodium for full-bodied taste and to soften the iron. Any hydrogen or oxygen in the blend was purely incidental.

Rainwater, especially after it collected in cisterns and became known as cistern water, had its devotees. When our neighbor, Gerald Frey, built a new house, he equipped it with a cistern, which was not unusual here. Most of the Freys, and their tribe was mighty, believed in cisterns. The Freys were mostly in the construction business and might be the only artisans left who knew how to build a good, round, brick cistern. Cistern water didn't need softening, they pointed out, and "it doesn't rust your pipes so bad"—meaning, in this case, the household plumbing. Nothing made hair shine better, not even beer. Cistern water also made billowing suds with less than half the soap normally called for. If everyone washed in cistern water, the problem of phosphates polluting rivers could be minimized exceedingly and the plumbing business would not be as lucrative. Beyond all these mundane considerations, the Freys liked the taste of cistern water and wondered, at the rate groundwater was being polluted, if it might not be safer to drink. It was definitely better than well water if you wanted a splash in your whiskey. Well water competed with the taste of good bourbon and turned your drink as dark as stump water.

How clean was cistern water? Depended. Cisterns were able to produce waters of interesting character if not clarity, especially when charcoal filters and screens were not properly maintained.

Running off metal roofs, rainwater was apt to pick up a tangy bouquet of zinc, which was healthful only in very small amounts. Cistern-water lovers claimed that the occasional foxiness of their favorite beverage was attributable to bird droppings washing into the cistern, or from a drowned mouse. These seasonings improved the water's otherwise bland taste and was no more harmful to the liver than a steady diet of pasteurized beer.

But narrow-minded urban-water lovers would rather put their faith in what rural folk scurrilously referred to as "city water." City water was about ten parts chlorine and hardly one part equally divided between hydrogen and oxygen. Trying to drink our village's water was like licking an old piece of barn siding that had been chloroformed in a gas chamber for three years. City water was "safe," although it was not clear what it was safe *for*. City water out of our Sandusky River was so generously endowed with various ethers of decaying organic matter and phosphates that it fizzed and foamed when shaken in a bottle. It might someday rival Perrier in popularity. Its effervescence had an added attraction: the delicate aroma of herbicides, which, according to Heidelberg College reports, the natives were quaffing right along with their chlorine and phosphates.

Carey village was luckier than our towns on the Sandusky River in this regard, as its city water came from deep wells that had not yet been contaminated with herbicides. There was however, local handwringing over the disturbing news that nitrate-laden surface water, from manure seeping down into the porous limestone subsurface, was contaminating the water in some farm wells. Occasionally the city wells issued forth a liquid the color of nearby Tymochtee Creek water, that is, the color of root beer, a mystery attributed to some form of iron in the underground strata. If it were allowed to age, Carey water clarified and was good for putting out fires. Tymochtee Creek water, if allowed to age, turned to mud.

Fine restaurants in Cincinnati added a slice of lemon to glasses of Ohio River water, hoping to mask the heavy content of chlorine, but all the practice seemed to accomplish, to my taste, was to dilute the subtle huskiness of blended asbestos, which had historically been "a fact of life" (or death) in the city's water supply, said the EPA. River raconteurs remarked that they had hoped, after the big carbon tetrachloride spill a few years ago, that the asbestos might be dissolved, but the spill seems only to have added a certain tang to the liquid.

Columbus, Ohio, city water got its distinctive taste from the abundance of nitrates with which it was laced, presumably from fertilizer running off the rich farmlands above it. Almost every spring, inhabitants are informed that the water exceeds the allowable content of 10 ppm of nitrates and that perhaps babies and the elderly ought to refrain from drinking it. The rest of the population is deemed to be so inured to cheap wine, homemade beer, and drinking Cincinnati water while visiting there as to be immune to any damage mere nitrates could cause.

Not as advanced as Californians, who could take a jug of tap water to coin-operated purifiers, urban dwellers in Ohio stubborn enough to actually drink water can buy bottled spring water at the grocery store. The bottled-water business is bubbling right along, the president of Magnetic Springs Water Company once told me. Magnetic Springs is a tiny village not far from our place, but its famed springwater is no longer sold by the company that bears its name, and in fact the company moved to Columbus. Magnetic Springs uses distilled water now and adds back into it food-grade minerals in proportions similar to the natural Magnetic Springs water so loved in the sweet bygone days—mostly calcium, a bit of magnesium, and just enough sodium to put a zing in the taste. "It's better than the real thing," the company president told me. He said that in earlier times it was the very poor and the very rich who bought bottled water, a fact he said he couldn't explain. I think I can. The very poor did not have access to *any* water, and the very rich of course wanted the healthiest water available, even if they had to buy it. "But now more middle-class people are buying," he said. "Sales would really spurt if Ohioans knew how bad their water was. They suffer under a delusion that if the water were not safe, the government would tell them so."

Grandpaw Rall had his favorite spring and suffered a kind of delusion about it too. He was fond of telling his grandchildren that even the reddish specks of rust in the water were good for a body. But he quit drinking the stuff when he looked closely one day and noticed that some of the reddish specks wriggled.

Other oldtimers swore by stump water, the brackish liquid that gathers in hollows and holes in stumps or at the base of tree trunks. It was good for whatever ails you, they said, especially if what ailed you was sulfur water. Another water of mystic powers was dew water. One of the long-ago Brodmans, my mother recalled—and she should have known because she was related to them—had the habit of rolling naked in the dewy grass on a summer morning to ward off disease.

Lest time forget, there was also quench water, the water in which blacksmiths dunked red-hot iron to cool it. One did not drink quench water, but it had a long-standing reputation for healing poison ivy. Acid rain might do that too, I've a notion.

CHAPTER 11 / *The Home Team*

When my neighbor, twenty-year-old Dave Frey, crawled out of bed one morning in August of 1984, he knew it would be a long time before he slept again. But had he known how long, he might have ducked his shaggy black beard and Prince Valiant head of hair back under the covers for a few extra winks. Or stayed there all day. Instead he went to the barn as usual, put in a day's work, nibbled nervously at his supper, and pretended to watch a little evening television. Finally at 9:00 P.M., when normal farmers think about retiring after a hard day, Dave donned a blue, gold, and white softball uniform emblazoned with the words "Country Rovers," climbed into his pickup, and drove forty-five miles from his family's farm to Findlay, Ohio, where our team was about to play in the Findlay Handicrafts Round Robin Slo-Pitch Marathon Softball Tournament. It was the big time to a kid who had played his softball and baseball mostly on the pasture fields of rural Wyandot County. Frey figured the Country Rovers, made up of players who were his friends and neighbors, had about as much chance of winning the tournament as the last-place Cincinnati Reds had of winning the World Series that year. By 10:30 he had arrived at Rawson Park in Findlay, where the tournament would start at midnight. True to his nickname, "The Worrier," he began to fume about whether the rest of the team would show up on time, even though they did not play their first game until 2:00 A.M.

2:00 A.M.? Marathon softball tournaments were not for everyone. The games began at midnight on Friday night and continued on through the weekend, one after another, day and night, come hellfire or high water. We had played when the temperature a foot above the diamond was 110 degrees and when parts of the field were covered with water. Almost all serious softballers get talked into playing in one marathon, but it takes hard addiction to the game to participate in a second one. For the Country Rovers, in their fifth year as a team, this would be marathon No. 4.

A roaring of mufflers and a musical horn blaring strains of "Yankee Doodle Dandy" announced the arrival of more Country Rovers. Like all the teams, the young men were loud and brash, whooping it up, modern trail-hands riding in off the range of their humdrum, workaday worlds. They piled out of their rubber-treaded steeds, the colors of their uniforms flashing in the overhead lights. Forgetting for a while the long week past and the longer one to come, days penned-up in cabs of grain harvesters cutting endless fields of wheat; days plugged into endless assembly lines; days chained to desks, store counters, gas pumps, or computers. For the weekend, they were not doctors, lawyers, merchants, chiefs; not rich men, poor men, beggarmen, or thieves. They were just ballplayers—knights riding into a strange castle, keyed up for a tournament. They were all a little crazy.

The younger Country Rovers were barely into their twenties, except Ben, who was only sixteen but could hold his own. Big Stoop unwound out of his Corvette. He had been throwing hundred-pound sacks of turkey feed around all day. Beside him came Tiny Tim, who weighed only 130 pounds. Sometimes when he caught a hard line drive at shortstop, the ball carried him out into left field. Out of the darkness sauntered my son, Jerry, who was quiet around the team. Having his father for a player-manager will do that to a person. Dan came with Jerry—Dan, who once

said, "When it comes to softball, even girls are way down the list."
Last on the scene was twenty-seven-year-old Steve, who just three
years ago was a rising pitcher in the Detroit Tigers farm system.
He decided that he preferred his own farm to any system. Steve
was even taller than Big Stoop. And his right arm was strong
enough, so the boys insisted, to throw a hound dog from center
field to home plate on only one bounce.

Jim, Ben's father, and I held up the old end of the team along
with stocky, bearded Chuck Hall, who wrote poems between
games, or if things got dull, during games. We picked out a spot
under some oak trees beyond right field in which to bivouac for
the weekend. As if in preparation for an attack by one of the other
teams between games, which had been known to happen, those
with pickups parked them in a semicircle around the big tent
Chuck was already putting up. Bedrolls, deck chairs, and sleeping
blankets were broken out. Someone went for ice to cool down the
beer and soft drinks.

The Country Rovers began the way most softball teams do: a
father and son not quite ready to bow to the inevitabilities of life.
It seemed to me that my boy, Jerry, was born with a ball glove on
his hand. I remembered him as a child forever dogging my tracks
carrying two gloves and a ball, patiently waiting until I stopped
work long enough to play catch with him. Jerry grew up watching
me play, as I had watched my father, an anachronism in these times
when parents sit on the sidelines cheering children.

All of a sudden, Jerry was sixteen going on twenty, about to
walk out into his own life as all young men must, and I was asking
myself, Why? Why couldn't we play together a few more years,
my old legs being willing? A solution presented itself. Our family
and my sisters' families were in the habit when our children were
little, of playing a savage game of softball on Sundays at the park
in Harpster, Ohio. These games, in which adults were known to
run down little children mercilessly in pursuit of a pop fly, were
the only Little League our kids ever knew. Babies came close to
suffering dehydration while their mothers were out in the field.

One of my sisters claims that she and her husband wore out two rule books a year, one from leafing through and one from throwing at each other. One Sunday after we had grown tired of trampling each other in combat, we challenged the 4-H club picnicking in the park to a game. Among the 4-H'ers were Dave, Tim, and Big Stoop. They moved uncommonly well, we noted. And some of our kids, Jerry, Ben, Jesse, Nick, and Simon for sure, did too. Why not join forces and get in a league?

We entered our first tournament without uniforms—four fortyish men and an assortment of boys, some of whom were actually too young for men's-league play. So inexperienced were we that Dave Frey insisted on wearing a pair of heavy workshoes, claiming he felt more comfortable in them. When we went out on the field to practice before the first game, a tournament official approached me and asked that we move off the field—a *tournament* was about to begin here, he explained. When I told him we were playing the first game, his jaw dropped. Our opponent was Groll's Furniture of Waldo, one of the premier powers in Ohio softball that year. They beat us 22–0 in five innings, using their substitutes. When we lined up after the game for the customary handshaking, most of our players had to reach up to grab the Grollers' outstretched paws. "It was like trying to shake hands with bunches of bananas hanging on a clothesline," Dave recalled.

Part of the reason softball is the most popular team sport in America is that a meeting such as that between Groll's and us was *possible*, if somewhat ridiculous. There are so many ways to play softball: slow pitch, fast pitch, or medium-fast pitch; with a twelve-inch ball, a fourteen-inch ball, even a sixteen-incher. Or with a stick and rubber ball, like our kids started out with. There are leagues for everyone: women, boys, girls, coed, and over-seventies. As long as a person can run, or at least amble, there is a place for him or her in softball. Spirit is what counts; skill is only desirable. And if you want to play in a tournament where you are totally outclassed, it's your funeral.

Softball players don't like being dictated to. If you like being dictated to, you can play baseball, football, and basketball in high school, college, and the pros. Softball players infuse the game with a devil-may-care, free-spirited flair that contrasts sharply with the disciplined rigor and solemn intensity one finds within the structure of "organized sports." The Country Rovers were exemplifying that now, as they filed into the dugout for their first game, whooping and hollering and frisking around like spring lambs. I had learned, for example, that as a manager, I couldn't tell any of them what to do. I could *suggest* that someone take a pitch, but whether he did so or not depended on the last motor impulse that crossed his synapses before the ball reached the plate. You just never knew.

"I didn't go out for sports in high school," Davy Frey once informed me. "I didn't like the way the coaches bullied the guys. It wasn't fun. Guys who thought they were going to get scholarships put up with that shit. Not me. I didn't want to go to college anyway." Big Stoop didn't play high school sports either. "I was told I was too clumsy," he explained dryly. Jerry laughed. "I didn't start growing till my senior year. I wasn't big enough to merit a second look from the coaches."

"Hey, you're lucky," said Frey. "Look at Tiny Tim. He still hasn't started growing!"

Dan stepped to the plate and began to go through his ritual. With one hand held loftily skyward, indicating the "time out" sign, he used his feet to smooth out the batter's box as if he were arranging a Japanese formal garden. Every pebble he disposed of, every bump he raked smooth with his cleats and free hand, right to the very edges of the batter's box. It took awhile. In our home league, narrow-minded umpires no longer allowed Dan his ritual, claiming that if everyone did it, a game would last two days. But in Findlay, there had not yet been time enough for the umpires to understand that. The catcher stared. The umpire stared. The pitcher fidgeted. By and by, Dan had worked his garden plot to suit him. He straightened up, hitched his pants, adjusted his batting glove, knocked imaginary mud from his cleats, spit, measured the plate with his bat, dug in his toes (thereby ruining the effect of his gardening), wiggled his butt, and took a deep breath, all the while keeping his right hand held high in the "time out" mode. Someone on our bench snored loudly, sending us all into a giggling fit. The pitcher was unnerved. He threw four balls in a row. That was our leadoff batter.

Dan trotted to first base with a Mona Lisa smile on his face. On base, he leaned over and wrote something in the dust with his finger. He never failed to do that.

"What's that guy writing down there?" the catcher asked Jerry, our next batter.

"He's making an arrow pointing to second base," Jerry answered solemnly. "If I get down there, I'll know which way to go."

Actually what Dan wrote was "WEIN 1", when he was on first. If he made it to second he would write "WEIN 2;" on third, the inscription would become "WEIN 3." "WEIN" was short for "Weiner," his nickname, which derived from "Hotdog," a common appellation for players who made lucky grandstand plays more or less routinely. Why he wrote this cryptic notation in the dust no one knew. We often asked him, but he only shrugged mysteriously.

We won our first game, a surprise for everyone since the opposing team was one of the better ones in the tournament. That put everyone in a zanier mood than usual. We piled into cars and pickups to hunt for a place where we could enjoy what most ballplayers really play softball for, the after-game camaraderie in a restaurant or bar. At four in the morning there was not much to pick from, but we finally found an all-night bakery with a lunch counter and plopped down around tables pushed together. Insults and idle chatter washed back and forth across the table. The waitress looked fearful.

"Sir," Jim announced, apparently addressing the player-manager, "as your accountant I must caution you that the hundred dollars you are paying to get into these tournaments is extremely expensive pro-rated to the few number of hits you get. It's costing you about $50 a hit."

"When did he ever get two hits in a tournament?" someone else opined. "I think he was 0 for July."

"I've got a new poem," Chuck served notice on us.

"Spare us."

"Thank you. *I think that I shall never see, a bat as lovely as a tree.*"

"Oh, Lord."

"*But since I have of muscles few, I think a bat will have to do.*"

Laughter gave way to a perennial argument: does the runner get to first base faster if he dives the last few steps? Opinion was divided. There was also no agreement on what to play on the jukebox. Or on which waitress was the cutest. Or whether the manager should retire from active play. The vote on that one was no. "If he devoted *full*-time to managing, we'd be in real trouble," Jerry said.

Back at the park, the eastern sky glowed pink. The park sat in a hollow rimmed by streets and highway on three sides. From the rim, the playing field appeared as an island of light in the predawn. A fog hung over the field, giving the game in progress, viewed through the mist, a soft, dream-like quality as if what was happening were not quite real, which was true. As the dawn light grew, the tents encircling the field appeared one by one, as if conjured up out of the fog, suggesting more than ever the memory of a medieval jousting tournament. From the oaks came the awakening songs of cardinals.

"Now I ask you," Chuck said, looking out over the field, "is there any sight in the world prettier than that? The Grand Canyon can't beat it. I feel a poem coming on."

The Country Rovers breezed through their next game, and as the hot, grueling August sun settled over them, they methodically won three more. No one slept. A few tried but were awakened immediately by giggling teammates. They were on a roll now, in the way a ballteam could get, some edge of advantage that psychologists have not yet defined. Jerry said it was the work of the softball gods and there was no explanation for it.

Carol and daughter Jenny, normally our scorekeepers, joined us by midafternoon, having taken care of the livestock at home first. Although softball was a game rooted in family, softball widows were more common than golf widows. Somehow we had avoided that problem. The manager's arch-enemy in holding together a good team was the uninterested spouse. Carol was interested because the whole family was involved, I guess. She brought meat from our freezer for the team, which, like an army, traveled on its stomach. I fried fifty hamburgers. They disappeared while Chuck and Tiny Tim engaged in a joke contest, trading seventeen stories apiece without a pause. We smelled victory and talk now centered on what we identified as our "fear of winning," which had so often snatched defeat from the jaws of victory.

With a lull in the games, the team found a nice air-conditioned bar where every play of every game so far was discussed in minute detail. Although only water really sustains a team in a long marathon tournament, and alcohol positively dehydrates, we succumbed now to beer. The player-manager was of the opinion that all good ballteams were welded together on a bar top, and he was now welding, pounding on the bar, trying to teach the finer points of the game, which he usually forgot to practice himself. Chuck was trying to outshout him with a rendition of his latest opus. The jukebox drowned out all conversation with a hideous cacophony of rockety-rock-slam-bang-hey-man-yeah-yeah-baby. The wives and girlfriends sat at a table by themselves, discussing babies.

"The defensive key to this game is to keep the opponent's runner" (pound, pound, pound) "on first base when he singles, not let him get to second by making a goofball throw to the wrong base. Then you can . . . "

"Softball players, a special breed,
Apart from the multitude.

Sacrificing love and life
For a seven-inning feud."
Rockety-rock-slam-bang-hey-man-yeah-yeah-baby.
"Then you can" (pound, pound, pound) "make that short throw
to second on a force, and maybe get a double play, too."
"Attuned to being vulgar, crude,
To swear, to spit, and chew.
Many think we're crazy.
Well, that helps a little too."
Back on the field, we hit a bad patch. Probably the beer dead-
ened our diminishing energy. What we needed now was good talk.
Already the team was five years old, and so we had escapades to
tell those who had not played with us before, or just to tell each
other over and over again.

The story most fondly recalled was the time Jerry almost
drowned in center field, and Frey could tell it best.

"Torrential rain had fallen the night before," he intoned, "but
the tournament officials were not about to give back the tourney
money and cancel it off. So they called out the fire department—
this was in Forest, and the place is so small you can get favors like
that done fairly easily if the firemen had a team in the tournament, which they did. They tried to *pump* the water off. I mean
this was a low-lying field, and it was one big *lake*. After three
hours of pumping, the lake had diminished down to two ponds,
one in left center and one around home base. They dumped about
five truckloads of Forest's finest sand and gravel over home plate,
which more or less got rid of the problem there. But then, and I
kid you not, they couldn't find home plate. You'd think it would be
easy by eyeing up from third and first. Just try it when home plate
is buried a foot below Forest sand and gravel, on a diamond that
looks like it was laid out by a drunk. They had to probe for home
plate with steel rods." By now everyone howled with laughter.

"So finally they found home plate and decided to play the
game, to hell with the pond in left center field. So there was a line
drive coming down over the pond, and Jerry was in full throttle

getting to it when he hits the water. Ever try to run fast in half a foot of water? The water tripped him up, but he made one last desperate lunge for the ball. He went almost completely under like a damn duck diving after a fish, and when he came up he couldn't breath. His mouth and nose were plastered full of mud and water, and he was coughing and we were beating on his back trying to open his air vents and all the while he was jumping up and down holding the ball up in his hand so the ump could see that he caught it!"

Tears were running down cheeks by now.

"That night was weird too," Chuck said, taking over as storyteller. "By then we were playing over on the better diamond in Forest. It didn't have water on the outfield exactly, just a big swamp out there. They had about enough lights on the field that if you put them all in one coop, the hens might not go to roost. One of those pea-soup fogs had settled over the swamp, and when a fly ball sailed out there, it just disappeared with the fielder disappearing after it. All you could do was listen to the squish-squish of running feet and a voice crying out of the wilderness, 'I got it, I got it!' Then pretty soon the ball would come flying back in out of the fog. No one knows to this day if those balls were caught or not."

By now the players were rolling on the ground, hysterically pounding the grass, remembering. That was the real reason that we loved softball so passionately—we would enjoy these shared experiences for as long as we lived. Even when I'm old and tottering, I'll look up every so often and see one of these young men, who isn't young either anymore, come to visit, and we'll pop a beer and live it over again, the kind of immortality that storytelling endowed. Where is there treasure more precious than this?

The laughter seemed to generate another round of energy, and by Sunday morning the Country Rovers were within one game of winning what for them was a big city tournament. We had one loss, the same as the team we had yet to play. Jerry was batting a sizzling .700, and every time he lined another single I was thinking of the hundreds and hundreds of pitches I had thrown at him in the backyard for all those boyhood years. Steve was right with him at .666 and Dan coming along at .550. Dave had rocketed completely out into space somewhere, getting hits out of bad pitches and making catches at first base that shouldn't have been possible for any human being. Big Stoop was pushing strike after strike over the corners of the plate, walking no one. The fielders were all throwing to the cut-off man or to second without being screamed at. It was awesome. In the middle of the night in a strange town, in the fifty-second year of my life, we had become a ball team.

Nearly delirious, we took to the field for the last game. The big bruisers from Toledo on the other team could have hit ground balls through my rubbery legs at third and won easily. But they didn't know that. And they had drunk a lot more beer than we had. We took a quick lead. They came right back. We forged ahead again, and again they caught us. Slow-pitch was so much a psychological game; a big lead often meant victory. But to come back from behind, to come back twice, as our opponents did, gave great psychological strength and momentum. And it was not like us to prevail this way through an entire game.

The top of our line-up was coming to bat in the last inning. We needed two runs to win. Could we do it after thirty-six hours without sleep? Dan singled. Jerry singled. Now it was up to big Steve, who would rather milk cows than pitch for the Detroit Tigers but who still wanted to prove a few things. To walk him intentionally would load the bases with no outs. So the bruisers from Toledo decided to pitch to him. Was it fatigue, too much beer, a kink in his arm, a pebble that he stepped on? No one would ever know, but the pitcher made a fatal mistake: the pitch came in square down the middle of the plate, honey sweet and home-run high. Six-feet-five inches of farm-hardened muscle coiled and unleashed. There was a flash of bat, too fast for mortal eye to see, and then the sharp, spanking ring of aluminum against leather.

The sound told it all. The ball hurtled toward tomorrow. Gone. The Country Rovers had won themselves a tournament.

We intended to go back to Upper Sandusky, home turf, and ride around town in a caravan, blowing horns and carrying on like a wedding party. But the drive home sobered our hilarity and made us realize how tired we were. Home again, the magic of the tournament and the tents faded away. Exhaustion sent us home to bed.

All, that is, except Dave Frey, the only one who had never gone to sleep, even for a few winks. He staggered into his house just as his mother and the rest of the family were leaving for a family reunion. Wouldn't Dave come, just this once, please? He'd missed the last four, playing ball somewhere. He could hardly refuse his mother's plea. He'd go a little while, he said grudgingly, get something to eat, and then come home and go to bed.

But everyone in America knows what happens at family reunions: softball! Wouldn't Dave play, please? After all, he was the family star. Dave rolled his eyes, and fetched his glove. As long as he was there, he might as well play a little while.

○

Subsequent events demand a bit of a footnote to this true story written in 1984. As time would tell, the Findlay tournament was not the culmination of a dream come true for me, as I thought then. It was but the beginning. My son and I would play many more years together because of my sheer good fortune in having a body that aged slowly. Over the years, some players dropped off the team and others came on. Dave Frey says that, according to his count, about 135 local men played at least one game with the Rovers over a period of fifteen years. But the most miraculous part of it was that eventually my nephews, Ben, Nick, Jesse, and Simon, grew up, came back from college to play with us, and proved to be as good as I knew they were way back in the Harpster days. My daughter married a ballplayer who was as crazy as the rest of us. So our team by 1994 was composed of seven men from our immediate family, and we were fortunate to have four other local boys, all excellent players, come over from other teams to play with us. In 1994 the Country Rovers came in second at the national invitational tournament in Canton, and in 1995, we won it against a field of 109 teams from Ohio, Michigan, Pennsylvania, New York, Kentucky, and West Virginia. Not bad for a home team from the banks of War Pole Creek. And it ain't over yet.

CHAPTER 12 / *The Homespun*
Sporting Life

The nice lady who weighed trucks in and out of the stone quarry proudly told me one day that she had gone home from work the previous evening and canned twenty-three quarts of tomatoes. I passed the news of that feat around the neighborhood but no one appeared surprised. Granny informed me that she had canned twenty-five quarts that same evening. "I always can more than I ever use and the cellar's filling up," she said. Then she shrugged, answering the question I didn't ask, "Beats me."

I had a theory. Our canning and freezing olympics was a game of one-upmanship that country people played to maintain status in the neighborhood. We ushered each other through our cellars of canned stock as if they were full of fifty-year-old homemade wines. (Some were.) The last time I checked the score, Pat was in the lead with 115 quarts of tomatoes put up already this year, and still more to go to make sauces and ketchup. Jenny, across the fields from Pat, was running a close second, having put up enough transparent applesauce to fill a bathtub, she declared. Marilyn, down the road from her, tried to top that with a tale of picking out fifteen pints of hickory nut kernels from the shells since last fall, only to be one-upped by Otto across the road who said that he had picked out twenty pints. This is like batting .400 in the major leagues.

At least this sport had some saving grace. When the season was over, you could feast all winter on your score, no broken bones, steroids, or disgruntled bench sitters on the team. Certainly civilization will arrive full-blown only when the headline "Pete Rose Cracks Hit No. 3,000" is superseded in historical importance by "Otto Binau Cracks Hickory Nut No. 8,000,000." Or when I see in the local paper: "Smith Outcans Barnes 110-109 in Kitchen Thriller."

Out here in the rural countryside we were slow-laners for the most part, seeking our sporting pleasures close to home. Or at least I thought that's how we differed from our city brethren until I picked up a city magazine—the *Columbus* (Ohio) *Monthly* to be exact—and to my horror found that we had become mainstream. The magazine was carrying on about something called the "New Homebodies." The New Homebodies appeared to be aging Yuppies to me, but the magazine called them "Retros." Retros went home after work, liked to eat meatloaf, grow gardens, read books, and rent movies to watch on weekends. Sound familiar? They played golf and softball, or a slow tennis game, if playing did not require much traffic-jammed travel, but they rarely jogged, power-walked, played racquetball, or *aered* their *obics*. Nor did they join many movements to improve the world beyond their backyards, where they were painfully aware of enough improvements awaiting their efforts to last the rest of their lifetimes. Retros, in short, had discovered how backsliding country people have been living for years.

But Retros had a long way to retro if they wanted to get back as far from the fast lane as us Old Homebodies. You would not guess in a hundred years why the sky was lit up over the village of Wharton (population 500 maybe) into the wee hours of the morning in summertime, no matter how thick the mosquitoes. No, it was not an all-night softball tournament, although that's a good guess. Wharton happened to be the center of the most rabid croquet tournaments in the Corn Belt—and I say that with some assurance because I believe it was the center of the *only* croquet tournaments in the Corn Belt. Why croquet, on professional, sand-packed, lighted courts, was a serious sport in this tiny village for fifty years, and most likely a hundred years if village lore is accurate, is a mystery no one tries to solve. Jack Opper, Wharton's leading aficionado of the game, said it was always thus. He remembered being allowed to watch the oldtimers play when he was a kid. "I was fascinated by the strategy. Real croquet is a very intellectual game, a cross between billiards and golf."

When World War II came along, the younger players went away to war and the old ones died off. Croquet lapsed for a while, was revived in the 1950s, then simmered down in the 1960s, when the court behind Sam Corbin's garage was closed. In 1984 the village elders decided to install two courts in the park. Opper laid them out and worked up a set of rules from the memories of the old-time Wharton players and the encyclopedia. "But with some of our own variations," he said. Now in the late 1990s, the game seems to be going into another simmering stage.

The mallets the players used were unique to Wharton. Most of them came out of Bob Coakley's workshop. The handles were much shorter than those on the mallets you see in the typical backyard game. The players had to bend over until they appeared to be searching for nightcrawlers. Coakley's handles were almost always ash, the mallet heads rock maple or preferably white oak from an old barn beam. He turned the mallet heads on his lathe down to the precise micron he desired, then slipped a heated stainless steel ring, cut from a discarded exhaust pipe, over each end. As the steel cooled, it shrank tight against the wood. "I learned how to do that when I was a kid," Bob once told me. "I watched my grandfather, Emmanuel Drummond, shrink steel rims on wagon wheels in his blacksmith shop." Coakley finally added the touch to his mallets that made them stand out in crowd: he put a strikeplate of aluminum over each end, making the mallet head almost impossible to splinter. A Coakley mallet should last a few days after forever.

The lights over the horseshoe courts at the fairground outside Upper Sandusky, or those at the softball park in Sycamore, often burned into the wee hours of a midsummer night's dream too. Pitching horseshoes was not taken lightly around there, the players readying themselves all summer for the grim tournaments that marked Fair Week. Miller Bowen, my neighbor, had been one of the stalwarts of the pits all his life. For years, I could hear the clank of his ringers echoing up the road on the quiet evening air. And when the sun went down, he drove out to the fairgrounds and kept on pitching under the lights. He slowed down a little as he approached his ninetieth year. Afraid to take his bicycle on the road because his sense of hearing was diminishing, he rode an exercise bike in his basement. "The odometer says that I've pedaled clear to California and over halfway back," he said proudly.

I doubted that the summer pleasures of our rural community were any more unusual than those of other rural areas. It was only that I had lived here long enough to see deeply under the skin of our existence and understood that the wonders so many people traveled the world to find were all in the place where one lived, if only we would really *live* there.

Driving near our little village of Nevada on a Sunday afternoon in summer, I thought I had slipped through some time warp into the last century. A surrey approached me, pulled by two sprightly Morgan horses. The people in the carriage looked vaguely familiar but were dressed in Victorian finery—a family of 1890 out for a Sunday airing. The riders turned out to be the Tschantzes, who invited us to their annual horse show on their farm, where they displayed their collection of horse-drawn vehicles and gave a short history of "the good old days." (They really were good old days from the viewpoint of rural society, all things considered.) John Tschantz later invited my wife and me for a summer-evening buggy ride through Nevada village and down quiet country roads around his farm. At one peaceful spot, surrounded by cornfields, he pulled to the side of the road and mysteriously told me to fetch out what was in the box under my seat. I pulled forth a picnic basket. Under the fine linen cover were three cut-glass goblets and a bottle of champagne.

The strangest "sporting pleasure" I've ever watched occurred right in our own barnyard in much younger days. Eddie, the star of our softball team back then, had pulled into the driveway on his International Farmall tractor and was jawing away at us about the game the night before—Dad was our manager. Noticing our Cockshutt tractor parked alongside the barn, he allowed as how it was "the most humungous pile of junk ever to come throm a thactory." (He had trouble with his f's but was using the word *humungous* years before it became thasionable among New York journalists.)

"It'll outpull that bucket of bolts you're settin' on," Dad snorted.

I found a log chain and hitched it to both drawbars. The tractors edged ahead in opposite directions, the chain tightened between them and the tires ground ruts in the barnyard gravel. Neither machine gave an inch. Then my father and Eddie decided that the way to determine which one had more pure power was to see which could move *slower*. That would indicate which tractor was geared lower and hence provide, they reasoned, an objective standard to judge which could pull the most, all other things being equal. So began the strangest race in history. Both tractors crept across the barnyard in low gear, throttled down till forward motion could be discerned only by gazing at the immobile barn behind them.

"Haw haw! You're going thaster. See?"

"Am not! You're holding your brakes down."

Time crawled by as each farmer feathered his controls to maintain absolute minimum speed.

"This is going to take thorever."

"No, it ain't. That Farmall is about to stall if you don't give it a little gas, and that'll mean I win."

"Tharmalls never stall."

But just then, it sputtered and died.

"Hoooeeee! I told you so!"

"Thuck."

But of the more common sporting pleasures of the neighborhood, hunting surely ranked at the top in popularity. We hunted an amazing variety of things, including plants and inanimate objects. Morel mushroom hunting occupied nearly everyone during the first two weeks of May. Hunting Indian artifacts held the same people in thrall from March to May on the bare fields of last year's corn and bean stubble before spring cultivation and planting to a new crop. Hunting game animals began in September with squirrels and ended with the last of the rabbit season in late winter.

It would be difficult to convey to those (usually urban) who view hunting and trapping with revulsion how much enjoyment traditional country people derived from these sports. Many families depended on wild game for part of their meat supply; many farm boys and girls depended on trapping mink, muskrat, and raccoon for their Christmas spending money. The thought that we might be endangering wildlife populations or that we were being cruel to animals never entered our minds. My mother, a saintly and kindly woman, was fond of telling how, as a child, she loved to track rabbits in the snow. When the tracks entered a tuft of grass in the field and did not emerge from the other side, she smote the hideout with her trusty club, either killing the rabbit or scaring it half to death. We routinely killed and butchered pigs and calves and chickens. Somebody had to. We watched raccoons claw bluebirds from their nests and hawks plunge their talons into quail. If we killed too, we only mimicked the food chain's terrible need to feed itself. In fact, we had ample evidence that if we did not hunt, wild animal populations would explode and cause problems for both farmers and other wildlife. A standard farm cliché said that "if it's nighttime, the coonhunters own it." Seldom was that rule challenged, not even when the hunters cut holes in fences to let their dogs through because coonhunting kept the population of raccoons, one of the most destructive and persistent of wildlife on farms, at manageable levels.

But even without these considerations, the skilled hunter was held in esteem most of the time. It was not easy to track a fox, stalk a deer, trap a mink, or train a dog to tree raccoons regularly.

These sports demanded discipline, stamina, knowledge, great powers of observation, and marksmanship. Fox hunting was especially revered because taking foxes required the greatest savvy. There were old hunters I knew who would track a fox all day, but when the chance finally came to shoot the cunning adversary, they would instead smile and go home to track the fox another day.

But sometime into the sixties, that kind of reverence for skilled, artful hunting began to wane. The traditional hunters gave way to the callous slaughterers who, from pioneer times, wished only to kill something in the easiest possible way in the quickest possible time with the least possible amount of discomfort or risk. Finally in our neighborhood of flat, mostly open squares of 640 acres bounded on all four sides by roads, fox hunting declined from a more or less "intellectual" and solitary sport to a brutal affair where a group of men and boys, taking the place of the hounds of England, chased a fox from one square to another, a new group taking over when the present group tired, keeping track of the "hunt" by radio in cruising pickup trucks and airplane overhead, until the fox literally collapsed from sheer exhaustion and was shot.

When I was a child, deer were non-existent here, but by the time I was fifty-five, in 1987, there were more of them than in the days when the Wyandot Indians ruled this land. Their reappearance was a source of awe and wonder. The sight of a whitetail running could cause a sort of intellectual orgasm. The animal's unbelievable agility and grace surpassed belief. From a standstill in the middle of a country road, a startled deer could spring over the roadside fence thirty feet away in a single leap. A buck in his prime could run at forty miles an hour for short bursts, and cruise ʈoken ground at thirty miles an hour for several miles at a , taking great elegant bounds that downhill might cover fifty feet each. Fluid drive. Or he might move at a nimble can- ɔting periodically into high bounds that could clear a seven- ʌdfall without hesitation. If it suited his purpose, he could ɩder a fence or a downed tree, given no more than twenty f clearance. Even standing still, deer evoke such awe in the human that seasoned hunters will shake uncontrollably with buck fever, go rubbery in the legs, even slump limply to the ground. Or they might fire wildly over the deer in an almost deranged panic they later could not explain.

Eventually deer were hunted in a manner similar to the way foxes were dogged down, with gangs of hunters driving the deer across the 640 acre squares toward shooters along the roadsides. Gang-hunting deer was seldom as grim and brutal as it sounds, however, because, as bowhunters contend, an older deer had a somewhat higher I.Q. than the average gang hunter. Man-smart deer couldn't be driven. They invariably slipped back through the line of drivers in wooded terrain or just stood still in the brush rather than break into the open, hiding themselves in amazingly small amounts of cover so that inexperienced hunters even very close to them passed by unaware. Consequently, gang hunters almost always "harvested" (one could no longer say "kill") button bucks, who were inclined to wander away from their mothers more than doe fawns and so were left without wise guidance and blundered ahead into the shooting gallery's range.

Another reason gang hunting was not a grave danger to deer was that a gang hunter usually joined the hunt for the camaraderie. If he (rarely she) carried a gun at all, he presented a greater danger to fellow hunters than to the deer. He spent most of the time shivering on the roads around the fields or warming up in a parked truck listening to the football game on the radio. If by some stroke of luck he got a shot, he more often than not missed, a fact he secretly rejoiced in; if he actually killed a deer, everyone would find out he didn't know how to dress it out. The point of most gang hunts was to laugh a lot, tear around in trucks chasing the deer, and then retreat to a favored bar or kitchen to brag about the afternoon's exploits.

The deer had more to fear (though not a whole lot more) from hunters who set up camps for a weekend of focused hunting from tree stands. In a camp of, say, five weekend hunters, one might be classified as a Serious Hunter, a second trying hard to become a

Serious Hunter, and three people who just wanted to get away from their normal routine. One of these three, a male, would invariably become the camp cook, although he refused to touch a dish at home. He stayed in the tent, a little awed and alienated by the natural world outside. He usually turned out to be a fairly good cook. A fourth person hunted the first morning, then settled down to tinkering with the portable TV, trying to fix the focus to bring the ballgame in clearer. In the evening he persuaded the others to play poker. He lost $50 every year. The fifth member of the camp was a "guest," a first-timer who had borrowed the Serious Hunter's old gun and had to be instructed on how to fire it. In the woods, he whistled, stumbled and thrashed around, dropped his coffee cup out of the tree stand, and shouted when he got lost. Quite often he was the only one to see a deer up close, and sometimes he actually shot one.

The Serious Hunter usually graduated from gang and camp hunting to the solitary trail, becoming interested only in trying to kill big-rack trophy bucks, and finally in trying to kill them only with bow and arrow or musket. He would make the long trip back to real sport hunting, where the quarry had a chance, just one step shy of going after the deer "naked with a knife," as anti-hunters said hunters should do if they were *real* sportsmen. Those who achieved success at bowhunting big bucks this way said there was no thrill like it. Roger Rothhaar, who lived in the next county and who had written a book about bowhunting trophy bucks once said to me: "I have hunted all kinds of big game all over North America, and the white-tailed deer is by far the most challenging. And they are all around us right here, in our home woodlots, in our home fields, very often right in our yards."

To hunt wary old trophy bucks successfully, solitary, dedicated deerhunters resorted to very tedious and stealthful efforts. They abstained from eating meat for a week before going hunting, like the Wyandots and Delawares did, believing that deer could smell the difference between a carnivore and a vegetarian. Another theory held that deer were getting smarter because the stupider ones got killed first and so did less breeding. Whether true or not, deer were learning to look up in trees for deer stands. Days before the actual hunt, serious bowhunters scouted out the major trails, feeding grounds, and bedding places of a resident herd. They studied the way air currents behaved in different wind directions, so that they could evade the deer's keen sense of smell to get close enough for a bow shot. They noted where the bucks rubbed bark off trees and where they pawed bare spots on the ground. On these scrapes, during breeding, the bucks were most vulnerable to the hunter because they were thinking sex, leaving their scent as an open love note to the does. The hunters, juggling all this information, selected the trees in which to build their stands and waited. And waited. Days might go by. To get to and from a stand undetected, hunters brushed bare spots in the leaves for their feet to trod on so as not to make a rustle. To approach a woodlot from a cornfield, they removed the lower leaves from two rows of corn so they could crawl along soundlessly. In their tree stands, and perhaps around them, they clipped away branch tips to get clear shooting alleys in all directions. Then they might allow a particular buck that came within range to walk by unharmed because its rack of antlers weren't yet of trophy size. I knew one hunter who watched and waited three years for a buck to mature and finally grew so familiar with it that he couldn't shoot it at all.

There was another reason for hunting trophy bucks (or, for that matter, cunning old foxes who have survived to the prime of life) that hunters themselves rarely articulated. The successful trophy buck hunter, especially the bowhunter, was with a few notable exceptions, a middle-aged male. Younger people either had not yet learned the patience for regular success at this artful, difficult kind of hunting or had not yet been able to order their lives so as to have the extensive free time necessary. Or they might simply lack the will to expend the necessary effort.

What the middle-aged male pursued was the middle-aged buck, and between them were certain similarities that belied the charge of anthropomorphism. As the big buck passed through his prime years, the constant wariness that had kept him alive against an army of hunters, wolves, coyotes, and wild dogs began to take its toll. He sought, above all, security. More and more, he lingered alone, away from the hunted herd. Or ran with other old bucks. More and more, he was willing to let the foolhardy younger bucks play most of the mating game, exposing themselves to the hunter's deadly aim. Only at the peak of the rut, when the moon was just right and the wild night winds blew, would he come to the rutting scrapes to claim his dominance or be driven back by a younger buck. If the latter, let it be so. He retreated to the deepest fens of the woods, as far from the man-smell as possible, there to dream of endless feasts of white cedar boughs and apples.

The middle-aged man understood. He searched for the trail of the big bucks driven by a similar aging process. Where to now? he asked, as he studied the hoofprints, as much of himself as of the buck. The man's offspring, like the buck's, had gone to find their own bedding grounds. If the man and his mate had remained lovingly together, hardly the rule, what was there between them but an enduring patience, except occasionally when the moon was right and the night winds of the soul blew wild? Solitude took on certain pleasures not appreciated in earlier years. The deep woods beckoned. The days of senility were just down the trail, perhaps waiting behind that beech tree already in sight.

The haunting, hunting question: Was it so bad to die now, still able to race at forty miles an hour, white tail flashing, antlers glistening in the sun? Or to wither and shrink into mangy feebleness, fair game for any stray dog?

Likewise, would it be so bad to die now, a hunter, still strong enough to draw seventy-five pounds on the bowstring and hold it steady, full drawn, without a tremor? Surely that was better than to suffer the slow, humiliating slide into the old folks' home. The bow came up. The bowstring tightened. The haunting, hunting questions, for the moment, vanished. *Release!*

○

The county fair became the culmination and celebration of all our sporting pleasures. There we institutionalized our competitive craziness into blue-ribbon battles over vegetables, fruits, wine, horses, cows, sheep, hogs, chickens, rabbits, quilts, paintings, carvings, photographs, flowers, cakes, pies, candy, cookies, jams, jellies, mud wrestling, horse pulls, greased-pigs chases, and even a chicken flying contest, all of us seeking recognition, that allure that was even stronger than sex. It was possible, in fact highly probable, for an Old Homebody to spend a late-summer weekend by rising at dawn on Saturday to go fishing or swimming in a farm pond, arrive at the fair in time to win a blue ribbon in English saddle riding, take a ride on Dave Pahl's beautiful horse-drawn wagon made of black walnut, enter the log-sawing contest, slip out to the golf course or the shuffleboard courts in the park for an early evening game, and then return to the fair to watch a favorite trotter win or lose on the racetrack. For those who could drag themselves out of bed the next morning, there were church services to attend, at the fair if not at church, followed by collecting another blue ribbon for the biggest sunflower. Then it was off to the horseshoe tournament, a dash down to the park to see which team was winning the softball tournament in progress, and of course a quick trip to the farm to do the barn chores. Back at the fair, sure that I could not endure another hour of being an Old Homebody, I ran into Noble Goodman, my childhood hero, who won a state cornhusking contest in 1937 and, a couple of years later, led our little village team to within a game of the state fast-pitch softball championship. Still straight as a ramrod in his seventies, he approached me with a big grin on his face. "We're going to revive the old cornhusking contests," he said, excitedly. "In October. You be sure to be there now."

CHAPTER *13* / *Home for Christmas*

I kept walking to the east window and pushing back the drapes, knowing that the headlights would first appear from that direction, through the spidery trees of the wintry woods, heralding our daughter and son-in-law's arrival for Christmas Eve. A half hour ago, headlights had beamed through the driving snow, and I had heaved a sigh of relief. But that was only a neighbor braving the mounting drifts, not Joe and Jenny coming from a far city to celebrate the holidays. I thought of the road, surely treacherous now. Jerry, our son, had gone out to get his girlfriend, Jill, for our celebration and he hadn't returned yet, no doubt joyfully plowing through country roads with his four-wheel-drive pickup.

"I think the fireplace needs another log," Carol said, hoping to distract me from my pacing. The storm made me nervous; I made her nervous. She offered me a hot toddy, but I said no. I wanted to wait until the family was all together before relaxing. As I tossed another ash chunk on the fire (ash wood wet or ash wood dry, a king shall warm his slippers by), I mentally ran through the rituals which, over the years, we had added to the celebration of our Christmas. Was there anything left to do?

Both the black Defiant stove in the living room and the fireplace in the lower-level family room were well supplied with wood. Earlier in the afternoon, when neighbors had stopped by for a glass of eggnog and Carol's blackberry–black walnut jam cake, I had conscripted them to walk into the woods with me to carry back the yule log, a huge crotch of unsplittable oak I had saved for this occasion. We had rolled it onto the toboggan, dragged it to the house, carried it inside, and wrestled it into the back of the fireplace, where it was now a backlog that would last through the night and most of Christmas Day.

The last coat of linseed oil was drying on the cherry-wood ring box I had made for Carol. All day the woodshop had hummed with work as Jerry and I hurried to finish gifts for friends and family. We had to keep a wary eye out for visitors dropping by, throwing old sheets over work in progress when an unsuspecting recipient walked in.

During the morning hours we had made our rounds of the neighborhood, now a holy tradition, to gasp over the beauty of everyone's Christmas tree. We especially liked to visit the person I called The Inveterate Farmer because we knew coming up with a compliment for his choice of tree would tax our imaginations.

I. F. and his wife had never found it necessary to join the Christmas tree beauty contest the rest of us pretended not to compete in. They possessed not a shred of desire for social approval. For them, a tree would do if (a) it came from their backyard grove of white pines for free and (b) if it had at least six branches, preferably three toward the top and three toward the bottom.

I. F. made us promise on his porch not to laugh at their selection this year. We promised. We looked. We laughed. The tree did have the required six branches, but there was enough room for a wild turkey to fly between them. This arrangement allowed for quite a concentration of ornaments in the middle. I. F. explained that the tree had been trying its best to grow between two larger trees and was losing the battle. He thought he might as well cut it down and put part of it to good use. It reminded me of one of those bristlecone pines I'd seen in pictures of mountain peaks, clinging to life by one gnarled root.

"This is the most unusual tree in the neighborhood," I said

gamely. "But in all truth, you have not equaled the creativity you showed last year."

We all laughed again. Last year I. F. had simple whacked a long wide branch off one of his large pines and affixed it to the wall like an espalier. In its own simple way, it was beautiful, as indeed were I. F. and his wife.

At the homes of my sisters and brother, we exchanged little gifts we had made or gathered from nature's bounty—jars of jam; home-hived honey; homemade caramels; original poems, paintings, or photographs; hickory nut meats; wooden trays for holding an assortment of nails; handwoven scarves and throw rugs—each of us giving some by-product of our livelihood or hobby. One memorable year we all chipped in and bought a neighborhood cider press.

Back home, I finished up the barn chores. Because it was Christmas, I fed the animals extra grain and spread clean straw bedding extra thick in their pens. The barn radiated a Currier and Ives ambience in the soft lantern light as the animals sniffed the new straw appreciatively.

Momma always had said, with an amused, wise-owl look in her eyes, that in earlier times, the cows knelt to honor the newborn Christ at the stroke of midnight on Christmas. As our cow Betsy settled herself into the fresh bedding, I thought I understood how that folklore had arisen. She lowered herself first on bended front knees as if in genuflection, before flopping down on her side with a contented little moan. "But Betsy, it's not yet midnight," I said for my own amusement. She stared at me out of the infinite, dumb peace of cowdom. I almost envied her. Her daughter danced in the new straw and then, like a belligerent teenager, butted her mother. Betsy ignored her as patient mothers all learn to do.

The sheep, finished with their oats, knelt to sleep too—except for Bounce. As an orphan lamb she once had had the run of the house, in made-to-fit diapers with a hole cut in them for her tail to fit through. We were never sure whether Bounce became bonded to us or to the television screen, which she would watch intently while Carol or I held her. Marked for life as half-human, she bleated whenever we came into sight. She was doing so now, tearing back and forth at the gate of her pen, kicking over her grain bucket in her eagerness to get as close to me as possible.

"Preserve me from a pet sheep," Grandpaw had always said. "Only one thing more trouble and that's a pet pig."

Now as I peered out the window, I thought of one more Christmas Eve task. Maybe by then the children would arrive. Once more I put on my barn clothes and headed there, taking along the red bow and handlettered sign I had prepared. The animals were all snuggled in their straw, chewing their cuds, warming the barn against the winds that whistled high in the trees outside. Even Bounce did not get up. I sat down on Betsy's broad, reclining side, and flicked off my flashlight, mesmerized by an elemental peacefulness. Betsy swung her head around and pushed her nose against my arm. Katie the cat climbed into my lap. She sometimes tried to sleep on Betsy's back, but the cow had her limits. She would suffer me to sit on her sometimes, or young lambs to romp over her, or an occasional chicken to roost on her backbone, but no cats allowed.

A sudden thought came to me. This barn would not be such a bad place for a baby wrapped in swaddling clothes to lie in a manger. We moderns overemphasized the supposed superiority of high-tech home comfort. A Bethlehem barn just might have been more comfortable than today's home: no radon, no carbon monoxide, no lack of fresh air, no budget-busting and environmentally ruinous heating and power bill. Maybe Joseph and Mary had avoided inns on purpose. I certainly preferred my barn to most motels I had stayed in.

Reluctantly I stood up, climbed into the loft, and threw down a bale of my best hay. The aroma of June filled the air. Stabbing a fork into the bale, I hoisted it to my shoulder and carried it through the snow to the barn at the farmstead next to us. The neighbors had bought one of our cows, Taffy, and I had decided it would be fun to surprise them and her with a gift. At the door of their barn I stood the bale on end, wrapped the red bow around it and tucked the sign inside the bale strings: "Merry Christmas, Taffy." I was very pleased with myself.

Back at the house I renewed my pacing. "I think the snow's letting up," Carol said, hoping to calm me.

"Did you ever think how ironic life is?" I asked her. "It took us fifteen years to work our way back to the country, and ten more to secure our beachhead here."

"Don't you have any more presents to wrap?"

"Now, just when victory is complete, when I no longer must travel lonely highways all the time, and sleep in lonely motels, and fly in those insane metal cylinders hurtling through space, now when we can live in sanity, snug and cozy and safe, and not have to take our lives in our hands in holiday travel, what happens? We have to live through that insanity again with the children."

"Oh, you could fall down the stairs right now and break your neck," she said, rolling her eyes.

I remembered another Christmas and an incident that had made me forever leery of the driven life, no matter how tempting the money. My father and I were cutting firewood and selling it by the pickup load in those days, taking advantage of every opportunity a small, struggling, family farm offered for making a little extra money. A traveling salesman coming through town learned of our firewood business and ordered a truckload for his home near Crestline.

"But that's farther than we usually deliver," Dad had said. "I'm not sure our old truck will survive the trip."

"Charge me whatever you want to," the man had said. "I'll pay extra—whatever it takes. I want a fire in my fireplace on Christmas, damn the cost. Money I've got; it's wood I need."

Those words stayed with me. *Money I've got; it's wood I need.* We loaded up the old Dodge at dawn on that Christmas Eve and headed for Crestline, about thirty miles away. Our customer's orders were to "just stack it on the south side of the house." He wouldn't be back from his business trip until late that night, but his wife would be there, he said.

His residence turned out to be quite far out in the country, a splendid suburban home situated on several acres. As we pulled in the driveway, what riveted our attention, however, was not the palatial house but a huge, fallen tree stretched out across the back lawn. The man had enough wood for twenty Christmases free for the labor of cutting it up.

We knocked on the door and a woman timidly opened it a crack. We told her our business. She nodded, having had word that we were coming, but still fearful in her isolated grandeur.

She pointed to where she wanted the wood stacked, then watched from the doorway, one hand on the doorknob, as if fearing we might at any moment attack her. Two children peeked out the door. I finally could not ignore the fallen tree.

"Maybe we just should have brought the chain saw and cut that one up," I said, trying not to sound critical. But she caught the irony in my voice.

"Yes, it must look strange," she said, "to buy wood when there's a yard full of it. What makes it sadder is that my husband would enjoy cutting it up. But he must travel so much. He just hasn't had time to do anything around here. He wants so much to live the country life, you know."

"Do you like it here?"

She avoided my eyes. "I guess I would if he weren't gone all the time. If we could really *live* here."

I thought about that tree in the yard all the way home. That man not only had the money, he had the wood, too. *What he didn't have was time.* My life, as pinched as it was financially, was freer. Dad read my mind.

"Money isn't everything, is it?" he said.

I, of course, would eventually take up the money trail, but I never could obliterate that fallen tree from my memory, and as the years passed it only etched itself more sharply into my mind. The path I followed came to a final fork. Either I could invest myself entirely in a good, secure career from which there would be no turning back save death or retirement, or turn aside into the slower but less secure life for which I yearned. I remembered the tree and took, like Frost, the road less traveled by.

I snapped out of my reverie and turned on the radio, scanning for traffic reports. All the stations played music, and all of it was about snow and sleighbells, tra-la-la-la-la. Most of the lyrics were written for another age. The words made sense only to the countryside of the past. Modern families did not dream of white Christmases. They prayed for open roads so they could get home safely. Winter wonderlands were holiday nightmares. Grandmother no longer lived over the river or through the woods, but half a nation away. Oh what fun was it to circle O'Hare in an hour-long holding pattern? Or to sit on a runway for four hours? Or lurch through snow on a traffic-glutted interstate, begging the fates that there were no drunks behind the approaching headlights?

Headlights! It was Jerry, four-wheeling through the drifts from town, breaking a path down the lane from the road to the house. He and Jill came inside and made straight for the Defiant. Only a woodstove can comfort cold bones when the wintry winds blast away.

"It's easing up," Jerry said, plainly disappointed. "Snowplow's coming along behind us. I didn't find one car to pull out."

"What's the interstate look like?"

"Not too bad. We went a couple of miles, looking for Joe and Jenny. Traffic's slow, but moving."

I decided to have my hot toddy after all. Carol and Jill now had the table nearly set. The oven exhaled heavenly fragrances: our own home-raised standing rib, our own potatoes from the barrel sunk in the yard, our own asparagus from the deep freeze, our own bread from our own grain, our own apples in Carol's own lard-crust pie. If heart doctors would ever taste her pie crust, they'd never say another word about cholesterol. Nothing tasting as good as a good lard crust could possibly be bad for a person.

"Everything produced by our own sweat," I said, gloating.

"Well, you promised to plant a 120-proof Old Fitzgerald whiskey tree and you still haven't done it," Carol said.

Headlights. We all pressed faces to the window. The snowplow labored by, and behind it, a car whipped into the driveway and gouged its way down the lane to the house. We were all into boots and coats and out to the car. Joe climbed out of the driver's seat, a big, cool smile on his face. "One giant step forward for mankind," he joked, striding into the snow.

"We made it," Jenny cried jubilantly, throwing her arms around me. "Now I don't care if it blows all night."

We ate from the overflowing table until we could only groan. I loved watching the young people shovel down food that Carol and I had so painstakingly produced and prepared. We celebrated in our meal a Communion Service as holy as those taking place in churches all across the land. Understanding the biological chain of being, the interconnectedness of all life, we could say with all of Christendom, that this bread, this wine, was our bodies—take ye and eat in love and remembrance of the bounty and goodness of life.

I kept thinking how lucky I was: surrounded by a loving wife and children; all of us possessing good health; the world of art, music, and literature electronically at our fingertips. There was nothing more in this old world that I really desired or needed. Mindful of the bleakness of so much of human life elsewhere, I wondered about how guilty I should feel for our good fortune.

I decided not to feel guilty at all. What was happening here did not happen by accident. It was not funded by wealth either. It was planned and worked for with sweat, blood, and tears, not luck. Visitors sometimes spoke of our idyllic life. But when they basked in Florida, we cut wood. When they borrowed money for expensive cars, we banked the money it would take to own one. While they had played on weekends, we had stood knee-deep in cow manure. We ate healthful food diligently raised by our own labor without expensive hormones, antibiotics, or pesticides, while they paid the prices for whatever stores had to offer. We were not altogether lucky, nor was our life all that idyllic. We had simply chosen to pay our dues in a different way.

The meal over, we retired to the family room to exchange the gifts piled around the tree. The tree, cut fresh from our own grove two days ago, smelled huskily of spruce gum. We took turns fiddling with the fireplace embers, each insisting that *now* the wood was arranged to throw the most heat into the room. The joy of the open fireplace is playing with fire without being accused of playing with fire.

We worked through our gift exchange, saving homemade, special presents for the climax. One year Carol had made me a milkstool out of cherry wood, so pretty I could not bring myself to use it in the barn. This year she had made a skirt for Jill, a teddy bear for Jenny, golf club covers for Joe. Jerry had made Jenny and Jill lovely jewelry boxes with inlaid, handcarved lids.

I handed Carol the ring box at the very last. It may be more blessed to give than to receive, but it is also more pleasurable, and I think, in this case, more egotistical. The round box was of cherry, with tiny pull-out drawers of black walnut and a turned, decorative knob of walnut burl in the center of the top. All the wood came from our land. The burl had been too hard for me to turn on the lathe and I had given up on it, only to find when I had returned to the shop that Jerry, far more skilled than I, had turned it out beautifully, his gift to me. Now I explained to Carol how Jerry had saved the day and about the decorative inlaid little circles on the front of each drawer being of exotic but local woods: redbud, sassafras, even one of pussy willow. The kids oohed and aahed to humor me. Ah, but there was more detail. A secret compartment. Carol's eyes sparkled with delight as she tried to find it. Maybe she was faking her failure to do so, but the sparkling eyes were all that mattered to me.

Afterward we sat around the fire, unwilling for the night to end. We planned our strategy for the big hockey game the next day, if we could get the snow off the pond. For players, we could count on about ten young people from three of my sisters' families, plus two brothers-in-law and several sisters as crazy in middle age as I was, plus our whole family, including Carol. The hockey ritual stretched back to another era of country life, some fifty years ago, when all the land around was in small farms operated by uncles and cousins. Back then, when the ice was fit, all farm work was suspended and everyone went to Grandpaw's pond for the hockey wars.

My generation was the bridge between those days and now, the last of those old-time players still skating, still remembering Dad calling a halt to forking manure in favor of playing hockey. I had to tell once more, for the sake of the younger ones, about Uncle Pete's Old Hickory hockey stick carved from a second-growth, red hickory sapling. It was not much for maneuvering the puck, but it was hell on shins. I had to recount how Uncle Lawrence once drove his old truck on the ice just for fun, and how it slid sideways into the bank and broke one of the wooden-spoked wheels in half. Lawrence had us lift the truck off its broken leg while he put a piece of curved oak branch under the axle as a temporary runner and in such fashion managed to drive the truck back to his farm a mile away. Mine was the generation that abandoned that kind of ingenuity and independence for urban money, while the older generation slowly marched off to the grave. I thought the hockey wars were the end of a chapter of my life, never to return.

But an amazing thing happened. My brother and seven sisters did not move away, and I returned. And we went back to the hockey wars, country men and women raising another generation of players. Now I was watching this newer generation grow up and go to the cities, but I kept on skating, an old man, an anachronism, determined to keep the puck flying and the farmland singing until these young people realized the vanity that lured them away, and they too would come back to raise yet another generation to love country ways.

Drowsiness overtook us and we stumbled to bed. But sometime in the night I awoke. A sixth sense had whispered to me. I sat up. The house was dark. Completely. The electricity had gone off. I groped to the front hall where the pendulum clock, un-electrified, tolled three o'clock. With a flashlight I checked the outside thermometer. Five below. Out in the night, there was to-tal blackness. No farm light, no distant village light. Nature had wrested the world completely from mankind. Our house was a spacecraft yawing about the universe. I thought how unnaturally quiet the rooms were, only to realize that with all the electric ap-pliances silenced, it was *naturally* quiet. I thought of how desper-ate this situation had seemed in the blizzard of '78, when we had not gone back quite far enough in time yet to regain sustainable sanity. Now as the Defiant grunted contentedly with its stomach full of firewood, the inside temperature was eighty degrees. I went back to bed. Like a certain long-ago family in a Bethlehem barn, we could, at least for this precious time, all sleep in heavenly peace.

CHAPTER 14 / *A Buggy Ride*

I didn't expect anyone to take me very seriously when I made this observation, but I learned that the Amish were one of the most technologically advanced and worldly-wise groups of people in society. Few of us "English" were fortunate enough to get to know the Amish way of life well, even here in Kidron, Ohio where I actually saw a traffic jam of buggies occur. I had been so privileged to learn from the Amish because of a chance encounter with an Amish farmer that led to an enduring friendship—for reasons that were not tied particularly to his way of life or mine. It was just that under his straw hat and my ball cap lurked two brains that were remarkably similar, considering the circumstances. Among other things, we both loved nature-watching, softball, good food, and a funny story more than we should.

I used to wonder what was going on behind those seemingly somber, bearded visages that gazed intensely out at me from buggies as I whizzed past them with the strength of 300 horsepower. Now, having ridden in my friend's buggy (to a fancy restaurant to celebrate my birthday), I knew the answer: They were praying to God that they would get home alive.

Most of us outsiders either sniggered secretly at the Amish lifestyle or bubbled over with sentimental adulation of it. A fifteen-mile buggy ride over Ohio roads would cure both attitudes. With trucks and cars thundering down on us from all sides, and our lives otherwise at the mercy of an uneasy horse that could (from my experience with horses, anyway) bolt without warning into the path of oncoming traffic, a buggy became as harrowing as a roller-coaster.

David handled the reins and appointed me co-pilot. It was my job to man the brake lever, which sounded straightforward enough but wasn't. Going downhill—and in Holmes County you were always going downhill if you weren't going uphill—the buggy coasted forward, nipping at the horse's rear feet. Couldn't have that. So the co-pilot hauled back on the brake lever whenever necessary. But only so much, so that the horse was not forced to pull against the brakes. A good brake operator knew precisely how much drag to apply to the wheels and then exactly when to let up as the horse reached the bottom of the hill and began the ascent of the next. To do that while carrying on a deep conversation about reconciling technology with theology was more than I could handle, and David had to constantly remind me to brake and unbrake. But piloting a buggy while engaged in the rarefied atmosphere of theological discussion challenged David too, so it fell upon his wife, sitting in the seat behind us with my wife (they were discussing babies), to pay attention to the road.

I was convinced that we "English" didn't appreciate the way the Amish combined technology and theology, and so we often considered them backward. It was hard to see, presently, that when cheap sources of fuel and power were gone, the Amish might look downright avant-garde for having pioneered comfortable lifestyles based on renewable but less plentiful resources. Unnoticed by even the most environmentally aware scientific researchers, the Amish had been quick to pick up on new technologies in solar, wind, water, and biological power, while perfecting mechanical designs and methods that required less net power than we were presently in the habit of using.

David smiled when I said that. He doubted that many Amish had really thought about their lifestyle in that way. Their goal had been only to use technology as much as they could to ease physical labor without violating their religious beliefs against exploitation of nature and fellow humans. If in doing so they had inadvertently discovered a more appropriate and sustainable technology for the future of us all, that suggested some very, very New Age thinking. David was so amused at the idea of appearing New Age that he forgot what he was doing and started to run a stop sign. Fortunately, our back seat driver got him stopped before a truck hit us.

When the Amish did seemingly weird things like pulling their hay balers with horses rather than with tractors, they were reconciling technology to theology. Their religion, as well as their common sense, taught that tractor power in the field (some sects use tractors around the barn) would tempt them, perhaps beyond their moral strength to resist, to expand acreage, which in turn would mean competing with their brethren, driving up the price of land, and eventually forcing other farmers out of farming and thereby destroying their communities. This, of course, was the history of mainstream agriculture and why what little rural community existed anymore among us English was in debt up to its eyeballs. If our "economic" form of agricultural competition continued, I figured all the farmland in Ohio would be owned eventually by one farmer, but his wife would still have to work in town to buy the groceries.

Whatever way one wanted to argue the theology of horses vs. tractors in the field, I learned, while loading bales on a wagon behind David's horse-pulled baler, that the work got done just about as fast with horses and somewhat cheaper. The motor on the baler used less fuel than a tractor pulling it would consume, and motor and horses together did not cost nearly what a tractor to pull and power the baler would cost. Theology could be economically profitable, in other words.

The Amish were wizards at mechanical innovation, forced to it, so to speak, by the proscriptions of their theology. In their shops, operating on ingenious, diesel-powered hydraulic pressure rather than electricity, they could machine new parts for horse-drawn equipment that was no longer being manufactured. They had duplicated antique woodbending machinery no longer available. I once visited an Amish businessman who had amused himself by installing on his desk an electric light that was powered by a wind generator on his roof. To lift crates of vegetables drawn from fields by horses, an Indiana Amish family used battery-powered forklifts. The batteries were recharged with electricity from solar panels on the barn roof.

My friend David used solar power to charge the electric fences that held cows in temporary pastures. Amish theology said homemade electricity was okay, but utility-company wattage generated by dammed rivers, coal-burning, or atomic energy needed to be shunned because it came to the house in such easy quantities that the temptation to bring the whole crazy English world, including television, into their homes would be too strong to resist.

The modern forecart was the best example of the advance in alternative technology that the Amish had spearheaded. The forecart was a two-wheeled affair with a long, wooden horse tongue to which horses were hitched. Implements to be pulled attached to the rear of the forecart as they would to a tractor drawbar. Originally, the purpose of the forecart was to keep the weight of farm implements off the long, wooden tongue of horse-drawn equipment, since that weight added to the horses' burden. But horse farmers soon figured out how to equip the forecart with a hand-operated hydraulic lift, a three-point hitch, and either very sophisticated ground-driven power take-off systems or a PTO system powered by the latest fuel-efficient engines available. David was particularly proud of the new Mitsubishi engine on his forecart that would, he said, "run all morning on a pint of diesel fuel and so quietly I can hear the meadowlarks above its purr." The forecart had thus become the equivalent of a smaller modern tractor at half the price. Yet it met the theological requirement that it could move in the field only at the speed of a horse. So successful were the modern forecarts that several manufacturers were making them not only for the Amish but for other horse farmers worldwide.

A theology that inspired three-point hitch, PTO-equipped forecarts needed to be studied, seemed to me. Amish theology was in some respects like the Catholicism that I grew up with in the forties. Amish hymns sounded remarkably like Gregorian chant, which for mystifying reasons has become popular among the mainstream. Fans of chanting would go wild listening to hymns at an Amish barn wedding, if they didn't freeze to death first, as I almost did. But Amish theology had a different orientation toward the world than Catholicism, which was the reason I contended that these people are the most worldly-wise, in a literal sense, of all Christians sects (let alone Eastern religions) and, for that matter, of all fervid agnostic and atheistic philosophies too. The Amish were in much more familial and soulful intimacy with the natural world than most of American society. Although they seemed "other-worldly" to the rest of us, other-worldliness was not the focus of their daily lives. The earth mattered crucially in their theology. They believed that God directed them to be care-takers of the earth in partnership *with* the earth, not lordly rulers over it. While mainline Christian theologians were haggling over dogmatic issues such as whether faith alone could merit heaven, Amish bishops were out in the fields perfecting the use of clover in crop rotations as a way of meriting heaven. The Amish weren't interested in how many angels could dance on the head of a pin, but rather how many life-giving microorganisms per gram their fertile soil could support.

"It is true that our theology is earth-centered and earth-car-ing," David said, warming so intensely to the discussion that his wife had to warn him crisply from under her bonnet that if he got off the road another foot *we were going to tip over into the ditch!*

David seemed not to hear her, but the horse did. "If the Am-ish have anything to offer society at large," he continued, "it is our notion of a theology for everyday living. I fear that people in gen-eral have become too alienated from the land, from nature, from the *real* world. Creation has become something distant from them, has ceased to be a living part of them. This kind of alienation can influence even seemingly religious people to become exploiters rather than nurturers. Not using tractors in the field or foregoing electricity in our homes is no great sacrifice when seen in this light, especially when we can figure out alternative technologies that make our lives as comfortable as any. You still can't beat the warmth of a wood-burning stove, you know. We really do see God in the birds, in the plants, in the soil. Heaven knows, when the first warm days of spring roll around, we farmers almost do worship the sun."

He stopped the horse and instructed me, somewhat mysteriously, to open the gate by the side of the road and close it behind us. We entered a private dirt lane that ascended a hill and wound down through a little valley. We rode along then, shut off by hills and theology from piston engines, neon lights, storefronts, utility lines, and suburban clamor. The buggy had become a time machine.

We traveled a couple of miles on this Brigadoonish road, during which time we passed several farmhouses, all peacefully at rest in the lap of the nineteenth century. The loudest noise was the snuffling of the horse. Verdant fields of corn and alfalfa spread out around us, alternating with pastures full of cows and horses, with here and there a woodlot growing timber for future barns and houses. The farmsteads were neat and prosperous. Peace and plenty reigned. Every vista my eyes rested upon suggested a George Inness painting. This was what we had given up for Wal-Mart.

The road went right through a barnyard, house on one side, barn on the other. The historians who claimed Currier and Ives depicted an idealized world that never existed should have been here now. Mother and children, busy in the garden, smiled and waved at us. Father, harnessing a team of horses in front of the barn, shouted a friendly greeting.

David knew that I'd be pleased beyond words, and he watched my awed face with pleasure. The experience of this secret road and its secluded little world was his birthday gift to me. "These people need not worry about a theology for living," he said. "They are living it."

CHAPTER 15 / *Alone with My Thoughts*

When I was living the nine-to-five ordeal in a city office, I could hardly wait to get home and rip the confining garments of so-called civilization from me. Off came the watch first, that irritating symbol of a handcuff manacling me to what Scott Nearing called the "oppressive wage slavocracy." Then away with the tight shoes and the choking tie, both apparently inventions of some misanthrope. If I were alone, sometimes my stripping did not end until I was stark naked, collapsed in an easy chair, imagining that my blood pressure was coming down to healthful levels. I didn't know if the lack of clothes was in itself soothing and comfortable, or if my nudity was a statement of something more significant: that here in the privacy of home, alone with my thoughts, I could be completely and purely myself.

I came to believe that much of the dissatisfaction that affected me, and evidently others I knew, stemmed from a curious side effect of "modern life": most people do not get the amount of privacy and solitude that their psyches crave because they do not live at home anymore.

Most people do not work at home. That means eight to ten hours a day, five or six days a week, they are surrounded by fellow workers.

Most people do not eat at home. That means that many more hours, once sacred time with one's immediate spouse and/or children, are spent in public places, often in tense "power lunches" or resplendent dinners whose sole purpose is to make an impression or keep up an appearance with business clients.

Most people do not play at home. That's another hour or so a day during the week and most of the weekend that is lived more or less publicly.

Most people do not pray or meditate at home, but have to impress their peers with their piety by going to a church. That means more public time spent mostly observing who's wearing the latest fashions rather than pondering the meaning of God and virtue. (Perhaps we should go to church in our underwear and suffer the humbling experience of showing off just how ugly and misshapen most of our bodies are. That might be an inducement to avoid gluttony at least, and, although it seems contradictory, adultery. It's clothes that make the human body seem lascivious, not nakedness.)

The only places where we might achieve a little solitude is in our bedrooms and bathrooms. No wonder Americans spend so much money to enhance these two rooms with luxurious extravagance. But most people keep such inanely busy schedules that they shorten their stay in even these two places to an absolute minimum (and even there, the telephone constantly intrudes), encouraging, among other torments, constipation and irritable bowel syndrome.

If people are no longer polite to each other, no longer tolerant, as sociologists say, could that be because of a lack of home life, a lack of suitable periods of privacy and solitude? Where people live more "lonely" lives, at some distance from each other, as in pioneer days, they tend to be more friendly to each other when they do meet. As a traveler I noticed that civility in public places increased as I went from more populated to less populated regions. Even between Minneapolis and Watertown, South Dakota, where I used to go with a cattle buyer when I lived in Minnesota, there was a marked difference in people's attitudes toward strangers. People "far from the madding crowd" appreciated com-

pany more, logically enough. But a bunch of humans jammed together would kill each other as rats did in similar situations. Road
rage was a desperate cry for solitude.

There is so much to be gained from regular hours alone. Only
alone do humans bring to fruition paintings, poems, music, books,
sculpture, artistic design of all kinds. How many more good works
of art in all fields would be created if people provided for more
solitude in their lives? How many more scientific discoveries and
technological inventions with *wiser* vision might transpire if the
scientist or inventor were allowed the solitude not only to make
new discoveries but to think out their possible negative effects
before a crowd of entrepreneurs rushed them into the marketplace?
Would not laws too be more wisely written and enforced if the
whole process were inspired and refined in quiet solitude rather
than submitted to the public arena of legislative halls and court-
rooms where hypocrisy and posturing reigned supreme? The world
has tilted crazily toward madness because the forming of public
opinion and the decisions radiating therefrom have been placed
on a public stage of play-acting, a vast video theater of the unreal.

The habit of the compulsive "team" approach to life was no
more pathetically visible to me in my nine-to-five days than in so-
called creative writing as ruled over by editorial staffs. When editors attended their very formalized meetings, which they did end-
lessly, the scene became just another public stage, a theater in
which underlings pranced and pawed their agendas before over-
lords in hopes of group approval—very much like a courtroom
only no one had to swear to tell the truth under pain of perjury.
Editors believed some synergistic magic would occur at meetings
to guide them to choose the right articles or books to publish. But
editors, as a class, exhibited hardly any interest in how to fill a
blank page with words and in fact had risen to their positions precisely because they did not like to write. They often told me so.
The bigger the magazine, the more people in the meetings and
the less chance that anything creative was going to occur. When a
great book or magazine article did appear, almost always outside

the "team" approach, the editorial staffs would shake their heads in puzzlement, hardly ever appreciating how *one* editor and *one* writer, having prepared themselves in solitude and then working *one* on *one*, developed the great article or book in spite of the meetings. When meeting plans did not pan out, the team could always spread the blame: "Well, we all supported this dud, remember." No great work of art, no great scientific discovery ever originated in a committee. Committees are good only at marketing mass products to mass consumers. And at making war.

Not only do art and science begin in solitude, but their beauty can be appreciated only in solitude. Reading a book or listening to music is essentially a personal, solitary experience before it can be anything else. One really grasps science, as for example in the theories of evolution or relativity, only alone, shucking off, as one would clothing, the intellectual garb one had been dressed in since birth. How many more people might gain deeper insight into life and into themselves if they had more time alone, where they could risk intellectual nakedness with the wisest and most beautiful expressions of art and science? Understanding the universality of Self, which is what art is about, and what science should be about, we might be inclined to treat ourselves and others and new ideas more kindly. Groups, in self-preservation, almost always reject new art and science.

The tendency to group is, of course, human. Loneliness is a terrible pain. But what has happened in modern times to carry us to the opposite extreme, to regiment ourselves into goosesteppers? Television is blamed for everything, but how can it provoke groupiness? It seems rather that the popularity of television is an effect of too much groupiness rather than a cause of it. A television screen shedding its seductive glow into a room full of people relieves them of the necessity of talking to each other, of even taking into account that others are present. In the glow of the television, people may find a sort of eerie solitude.

Perhaps modern society's curious rejection of the solitary life has been mainly a result of the extremities to which we have pushed schooling. There are even classes for unborn children. If a child is not in some kind of school by age three, its parents are made to feel guilty. Preschool has become status quo; kindergarten was made obligatory under the law—something about teaching children how to get along with each other, the teachers, clutching their paychecks, told us. But it seems to me that what they are really teaching is not social graces, but the herd instinct in which one schooling method fits all. And so it came to pass that rather than living within a society made up of babies, children, teenagers, young adults, the middle-aged, and the old, as would have occurred at home, the school herd has fenced itself off in peer groups and become insensitive to the real social graces. They do not learn the greatest lesson: how to understand, tolerate, and love people older or younger than they, or people richer or poorer than they, or even, despite all schooling to the contrary, people of different ethnic roots than they. They do not learn how a society *functions*. Feeling alien to social graces, to the real world, they often stay in the dysfunctional test tubes of classrooms, amassing more and more degrees without experience in the life the degrees certify, creating a new elitism which is the godfather of totalitarianism. They often end up as "single parents," not realizing how that phrase is oxymoronic, not even learning how to understand people of different sex than they.

Caught in the schooling beehive of the seminary—the "priest factory," as real society often referred to it quite accurately—I escaped by sneaking away to a lonely stretch of a river, shucking not only bodily clothing that regimentation dictated but mental clothing as well, going for a swim, and then basking for a tranquil hour or more on a huge log overlooking the water. That log, that stretch of river, was the closest thing to a true home that I had at the time. And the closest thing to a genuine classroom too. I achieved more than a release from the considerable tensions in my life; the hours of observing river life, backed by reading books by other lonely observers, instilled in me a sense of the ultimate social graces that bound all living things in ecological sustainability. As I lay motionless on the log, neither wild animals nor the occasional human seemed to notice me. I smelled too much of the river and looked too much like the log, I suppose. A muskrat, an animal with poor eyesight, routinely clambered up on the log beside me and dallied there, seeming to drift with me to the edges of the unconscious. I watched an old male beaver, excluded between mating seasons from the family he fathered and protected, build, half-heartedly it seemed to me, a crude bachelor shelter in the eddy of the river. Once I saw on the opposite bank, a human couple mating, as heedless of all other existence as the two bluejays in a nearby tree doing the same thing. The human activity no more embarrassed me than the bluejays. All's right in the world, I'm sure Browning would have said. As the soft wind blew over my drying skin with the most exquisite softness, I felt myself slipping out of my own identity, my own persona, and gliding quietly into the flow of biological life around me, like the river itself. I came to believe, in hindsight, that those golden moments kept me sane in that trying period of my life. And taught me, forevermore, how to love all "creation."

CHAPTER 16 / *Home Villages*

I grew up accepting our tiny neighborhood hamlets as a part of the rural landscape. Just as I could learn fully the wonderful value of a family farm only by leaving it for a while and comparing it to other modes of life, so too I had to go away and come back to realize what fascinating artifacts of the passing agrarian society these little villages were, and how in an electronic age, they were becoming the almost perfect place to live. Harpster, hardly four miles southeast of Old Home, was a good example, being, by geographical default, without any economic temptation to grow. Once a local entrepreneur suggested putting an apartment building in Harpster, and the whole town rose in wrath. In this quiet, neat place of about one hundred houses and two hundred and fifty people, you were in walking distance of church, grocery, post office, gas station, farmland, wildlife preserve, and spacious garden if you wanted one, and able to bring the whole wide world of urban culture to your living room by way of electronics. Until about thirty years ago, you could board a train regularly in Harpster and be in downtown Columbus faster than you could get there by car today, and a whole lot more comfortably. This convenience will surely come again. Also until recently, village children could easily walk to school under the watchful eye of the whole community.

Closing the school was the cruelest blow to what a discerning traveler might view as another dying country village. But most of us who had lived in or around Harpster all our lives would not agree. We believed that if Harpster died, a debatable assumption, it would be because it was being slowly murdered by deliberate economic policies.

Not your typical, made-for-TV murder to be sure. This was murder the way war was murder, killing by social consent. Finding someone to blame was therefore no easy task. Upper Sandusky, the county seat, seven miles to the north, was the prime suspect in Harpster's murder, but Marion, ten miles south, was certainly an accomplice, and Columbus, sixty miles away, was definitely implicated. All three cities were draining away most of the money—the economic lifeblood—that once cycled and recycled several times in Harpster before it was finally gathered in the vaults of big city banks.

The murder weapon was the piston engine, which, in the form of automobiles, carried the people away to the city to recoup some of the money that had gone there and, in the form of tractors, melded little farms into big ones and sent the surplus farmers away too. That made U.S. 23 an accessory to the crime, taking traffic from the railroad, which was the reason Harpster existed in the first place. Sharing the blame were the communications media that had brainwashed the people into believing that paradise lay where the loose change jingled, amid the glittering lights of the city. The grain elevator was also an accessory, an unwitting weapon of agribusiness sucking up the corn, wheat, and soybean wealth of the surrounding land and sending it out to "feed the world" while the village declined. I stood in the village's last grocery store, the Killdeer Kwick Mart, and looked out the window at the tall grain silos. I had just paid a dollar for a loaf of "enriched" bread. I noted to myself that there were about sixty loaves of bread in a bushel of wheat. But for the wheat leaving the elevator by the trainload tomorrow, the Harpster farmer would be lucky to receive $2.70 a bushel, which hardly covered the cost of producing it. Thus, what

left Harpster at an unprofitable $2.70 returned as $60 of Colum-
bus-baked bread, from which the most nutritional part of the grain
had been removed.

In a murder, only the immediate deathblow is considered the
cause of the deed. When a person lamed in an auto accident is
later killed because he is unable to flee an assailant, the driver
who caused the earlier accident is not implicated. So in Harpster's
death, the local school district, which delivered the seeming deathblow by closing the school, received the brunt of the blame, even
though it was merely following the same economic philosophy that
had already put the village in decline.

"You have a gun pointed at Harpster's head," Cecil Dennis,
the postmaster, shouted angrily at John Berg, the new school su-
perintendent, a stranger brought in to do the dirty deed, during
the hearing over the issue. "If you close our school, you as much as
pull the trigger."

Berg pulled the trigger. Faced with the perceived necessity of
reducing the number of schools in the district to save money, he
advised the school board to close at least one country elementary,
and better two (but none of the three elementaries in the more
urban county seat of Upper Sandusky, a fact well noted by farmers). The board chose the latter course—shot Harpster and another rural school in Eden Township. "They really wanted to close
all four country elementaries," said Mike Morral, the mayor of
Harpster bitterly. "But that would have brought too much opposi-
tion all at once. So they closed only two this time around." A few
years later, a third one was closed, Salem Township, without a fight,
and it appeared that only a lack of space in the three county seat
elementaries was saving the fourth one in Marseilles. If history
continued to follow the trend, school officials would soon call for
a tax levy to build a new, in-town, consolidated elementary school,
forcing children to ride buses for hours a day and crowding them
into one big child factory, the way the hogs and chickens were
being hauled long distances and crammed into animal factories.

That comparison was appropriate. Even as the little neighborhood schools shut their doors, the local livestock markets closed, one by one. There was once a stockyard in Harpster. Both it and the one in Upper Sandusky closed in my youth. Now, with livestock to sell, I watched the stockyards at Carey, Arlington, Marion, and Kenton fade away. Only Bucyrus remained close enough for practical hauling. We were in the grasp of some awful monolithic, monopolistic economic power that was relentlessly destroying local independence. Local everything. Where would it all end?

In Harpster, people wondered if the life and death of their village really was "economic determinism," as conventional economists liked to say, or if the "fate" was deliberately willed. Vaughn Morral, who with his son Mike, the mayor, operated an excavating business from his home in Harpster, crawled out from under his father-in-law's house, where he was repairing a furnace pipe. As was his habit, he pondered the question of fate awhile, studying his feet. Then he nodded at the closed store across the street, which his father-in-law, Al Brents, operated for thirty-one years, and which, until a few years ago, had been in continuous operation for over a century. "Nope, Harpster isn't dying," he said. "It's being done in." He paused, studying his questioner's face for a reaction. "For one thing, regulatory red tape is chasing away businesses that small villages might otherwise get. In regulatory law, government thinks that one size should fit all. There was a buyer for the general store, a fellow who wanted to make it into a leathercraft shop employing six people. Perfect for us. But state regs said that he had to install a $20,000 leach bed to handle his septage. He went somewhere else. The existing septic system for that building was just fine for years and years with more than six people working in that building, and it is still adequate."

Jerry Gier, who owned the building, said he believed there were other reasons the leather worker didn't buy, but he agreed with Morral's appraisal in general. "Another fellow wanted to put a pizza carryout in the building, and the septic regulations definitely did stop him." Gier had since turned the old general store into a mini-mall for antique dealers, and he operated with his son, Jamie, a thriving smithy and metal-working business in the shop behind the store, carrying on the blacksmithing tradition in Harpster started by the great-grandfather of his wife, Sara. He would have liked to keep the general store going too, but found it impossible. "I was trying to hold down a factory job at the time and run the store too, and I wanted to get started in blacksmithing," he says. "It got to be more than my wife and I could handle at the time. But now we hope we've found a way to keep the store alive too. *I think what finally kills villages is a lack of love.*" I was stunned by his remark. I knew that's why farms died too.

Bob MacClaren turned off the Chopin tape he was listening to while building furniture in his retirement woodworking shop and also pondered the question of economic fate. As a young traveling salesman, he and his wife and children moved to Harpster from New England in 1947. When the company he worked for wanted him to increase substantially the amount of traveling he was doing, he quit. Harpster was as nice as any New England village he knew, he said, and cheaper to live in. He decided to stay. He started his own poultry and egg business in the old hardware store behind the general store. "No, it's not fate that kills villages," he finally said. "You have to work harder to make a go of it in a place like this, and it seems like no one wants to work that hard anymore. Right before I sold my egg business, I moved it to Upper Sandusky, which should have meant more opportunity because of the bigger town. But the man I sold it to went broke."

Al Brents had his own example of how Harpster was being "done in." "After I retired from the store," he said, "I worked for the bank that shared the building with me. Back when the Harpster and Sears families ran that bank, there wasn't a more solid one in the state. Cy Sears never lost but one loan, and that was for only three hundred dollars. Then the bank was sold. Some shyster in Columbus got hold of it and there was one blunder after another. [One of the people involved eventually was convicted of fraud.] They built a new bank building on the edge of Harpster, which immediately hurt the store because people who had come in to do their banking invariably had gone into the store, too. Then all of a sudden the bank officers' salaries took a big jump upwards. The local people got downright unfriendly after that. Eventually Commercial Bank, in Upper Sandusky, bought the bank, but then most of the business was moved to Upper. Now it's just a place to make deposits and withdrawals, and many customers who used to do business here have gone to other banks."

Why was the local bank sold? "The plain truth is that no one in the family wanted to take it over," says Craig Bowman, farmer and now the reigning patriarch of Harpster, and the fifth generation of the family that gave it its name. "When I came out of the Navy after World War II, I went to work in the bank with Uncle Cy, but I couldn't stand to be shut up inside like that. Uncle Cy was an amazing man. He'd stay after working hours, night after night. He went through every canceled check at the end of the day. He never had an overdraft. And he always knew when the bank examiners were coming." He paused, enjoying that detail. "I guess it's not that you can't be a success in a village, but young people with that kind of energy and talent will go to the city, where they believe they can be even more successful. You know, you have to be really clever to make it in a village. Uncle Cy and John Lavely did all right with the grain elevator. But the first guy who bought it from them went broke, and it has been changing hands regularly ever since."

If political and personal connivance, or at least acquiescence, rather than "fate" caused its decline, Harpster should perhaps not feel too outraged because that's how the village started. When David Harpster, the "Wool King of the World," as he was known as far away as New York City in the latter 1800s, heard that a railroad was coming through southern Wyandot County, he lost no time in offering the officials free passage through three miles of his sheep range plus a year's production of wool. That was a hefty bribe considering that his annual wool clip averaged 40,000 pounds according to old records, enough to fill six railcars. The bribe was extolled as public-spirited generosity and, of course, accepted. In 1875, Harpster and another farmer, John Wood, laid out the village, first called Fowler after another illustrious local farmer. So ended the Wool King's trail drives to Philadelphia and Baltimore. Legend says that in his earlier years, he once rode the whole way to Baltimore, sleeping and eating in the saddle, dismounting only to relieve himself. Legend also says that when he was served oyster soup in a high-toned New York restaurant at the end of a trail drive, he cursed at the taste and spit the foul stuff on the floor.

The birth of Harpster, the village, meant the death of Bowsherville, two miles to the west, where Harpster, the man, got his start, working in the general store until 1836. He eventually became part owner of the store. But Bowsherville's demise could hardly be blamed on Harpster village, since the former's cluster of hotel, general store, drygoods, hattery, pottery factory, and race track were already in decline, having been mortally wounded by the rise of Little Sandusky, the village one mile east of Harpster on the stage-coach line between Detroit and Columbus. Bowsherville was itself built on a kind of political connivance, its birth a result of the law that forbade selling liquor on the Indian reservation, which at that time occupied most of Wyandot County. By establishing a saloon just across the reservation border, wily old Anthony Bowsher (David Harpster's mentor) could carry on a lively trade with Indians and whites alike, making the town flourish until the Indians were shipped off to Kansas in 1843. By 1879, Bowsherville was not even listed on the county map, partly because influential Methodists of the area wanted everyone to forget the drinking and debauchery characteristic of the town, called in pioneer papers "the most ungodly place in the world." By 1900 the village had entirely vanished. Even the church, perhaps embarrassed by its sinful location, was lifted off its foundation and moved down the road to Pleasant Grove, another aspiring village long since vanished; eventually it became a machinery shed in Russell Manhart's barnyard, where it still stands today.

While Bowsherville died and Harpster scratched for a toehold along the railroad, Little Sandusky, which we locals called simply Little, flourished. A line of fourteen stages stopped daily to enjoy the services of John Rappe's famous inn. The usual accouterments of civilization followed: grocery, drygoods, livery stable, harness shop, blacksmith, doctor, lawyer, merchant, chief, church, school—the works. Farm boys riding into town for singing school, or an evening literary, or a church meeting, straddled a forkful of hay slung across their horses' backs so their pants would not smell like horse after the ride to the village and so the horse had something to eat during the festivities.

But by the late 1800s, Harpster was clearly into its ascendancy over Little. "Little tried hard to get the railroad," said Fern Erickson, who in her mid-eighties was the beloved matriarch of Harpster, coming back home here in her retirement after years of living in Chicago. "But Little's leaders could not match the wits of David Harpster. There was enmity between the two villages for a long time after." The enmity increased when Harpster became the site of the township elementary and high schools. So deep was the bitterness that when the schools in Harpster closed, first the high school in the sixties, and then the grade school in the eighties, farmers around Little Sandusky with deep roots supported the moves, a perfect example of cutting off one's nose to spite one's face.

Harpster village would have vanquished its competitor sooner if the highway through Little hadn't allowed it to compete somewhat with Harpster's railroad. Little had another edge. The influential Methodists of Harpster had strongly discouraged alcoholic beverages in their village. Many of the titles to the lots had deed restrictions against the selling of liquor on the property. It was not until the 1970s that beer and wine were sold in town. That meant that Little had little competition for its lucrative saloon trade down through the years. A farmer near Little told me that in the 1940s, when as a boy he was sent into the store to pick up the Sunday paper after church, "the place was already full of drinkers—'the godless,' as my mother referred to them. Of course they were mostly from Harpster."

That story made Al Brents laugh. "A fellow in Harpster once was bit by a rattlesnake," he recalled, "and his wife hollered to the neighbors for whiskey. All up and down the street, people came running out of their houses with fifths in their hands." He paused. "That's how dry Harpster *really* was. As a matter of fact, some of the best moonshine in the world was made during Prohibition down in Killdeer, not two miles from my store."

Eventually, after new Route 23 bypassed Little, its last two stores closed without a whimper. One of them was my favorite hangout as a 1940s teenager, where I went to act what I thought was quite recklessly, smoking cigarettes, drinking milkshakes, and scanning *Life* and *Look* magazines for any hint of a bared female breast. Even Little's Methodist church found times too hard to continue its payments to conference headquarters, and so church authorities merged the congregation with Harpster's. Interestingly though, Little's church did not close. Religion does not have to dance to the state's fiddles like education. Another denomination, younger, smaller, and willing to get by on less money, took it over.

As with Little, there was no historical date for the death of Wyandot, yet another village a mile further east, nor for Brownstown, two miles west of Bowsherville. The semblance of a village remained at Wyandot, but Brownstown completely disappeared, even though a hotel once flourished there, as well as a grocery store that did a lively enough business to lure Dillinger into robbing it. Scot Town and Pleasant Grove were sprouting villages between Brownstown and Harpster that had vanished also, not only from the land but from folk memory. The sad truth was that if one could animate a map of Wyandot County into fast motion, every year passing as swiftly as an hour, we would see villages springing up and dying down like weeds.

As Little faded, Harpster bloomed in its noonday, Victorian sun. By the turn of the twentieth century, it boasted a carriage and wagon factory, a drainage tile factory, a flour mill, a bustling stockyard, a grain elevator, a butcher and meat shop, a blacksmith shop, a shoemaker, and at least one doctor's office. The big brick "business block" that David Harpster built, which still dominates the town, contained the bank, the post office, a drygoods, and a grocery store. Across the street where the post office now sat, Colonel Cyrus Sears (grandfather of the Cy Sears mentioned earlier), built a hotel. Sarah, his wife, a daughter of David Harpster, did the cooking.

Although blue-collar and farm work were their preferences, the Harpsters, Fowlers, Searses, Woods, and Lewises in and around the village lived in a Gilded Age splendor hard for today's residents to imagine. Wool King Harpster's stately residence just north of town, built in 1871 for the then princely sum of $15,000, was referred to as the House of David, and there the family hosted grand balls, weddings, prayer meetings, basket "pic-nics," and extravagant Fourth of July celebrations.

Iva, David Harpster's other daughter, married wealthy William Bones of New York. As if the Harpster family, owning and operating some 4,480 acres in Ohio, 2,240 in Illinois, 600 in Nebraska, and 240 in Iowa, all "more or less improved and under fence," needed more wealth, Harpster's granddaughter married into the Fowler family, which, just east of Harpster, ran almost as many sheep as the Wool King. Iva Harpster Bones moved to New York, where she carried her childhood memories of brawling, raw Bowsherville to the highest social pinnacles of East Coast society. From New York, she ran with shrewd acumen the affairs of the Harpster village bank until 1940. "Iva wanted to come home. She and her husband once moved out to her father's mansion and refurbished it, but they did not stay long," said Fern Erickson. "Mr. Bones could not stand the isolation of rural Ohio, and they soon moved back to the city."

The highest point of Harpster's Victorian splendor was probably reached on June 30, 1896, when Charles Lewis wedded Francis Sears, the granddaughter of David Harpster and the daughter of Colonel Cyrus Sears. Charles's father, John, who took Fern Erickson into his home in the 1920s when she was orphaned, was an educator and the president of the Harpster bank. His second wife was a Sears also. Charles followed his father into the bank, published a local newspaper, and was elected lieutenant governor of Ohio in the 1930s.

The wedding occurred in the palatial home of the bride's parents in Harpster and was described in the paper at great length:

> The decorations were exquisite, consisting of ferns, daisies, sweet-peas, and roses, arranged by artistic hands adding grandeur and elegance to an already magnificent home. Braun's superb orchestra [local] furnished the music. . . . Among the many valuable gifts tendered the couple were two one-thousand-dollar checks, one from David Harpster, grandfather of the bride, and the other from the father of the groom.

To appreciate the value of a thousand dollars in 1896, consider that Colonel Sears's home was built in 1882 for $5000. Today, if skilled enough bricklayers could be found to do it at all, the house would cost at least half a million dollars and a great deal more than that in an exclusive suburb where such houses are usually found. It is today still an elegant and beautiful home, in a pleasant park-like setting, although incongruously, but fittingly enough, overshadowed by grain elevators nearby.

Over the years, the flour mill added the elevators, and business shifted from milling to storage and shipping. Across the railroad tracks from the bank and general store, a little restaurant opened after the hotel was torn down in the thirties. Shifting my wild teenage adventures from Little to Harpster, I often amused myself by calling friends on the old crank telephone still in service there. Craig Bowman amused himself by training his pony to go into the general store without balking, where the proprietor would give them both a piece of candy. A filling station eventually came to town, followed by an auto repair shop and even a Ford dealership. Then Bob MacClaren started his poultry and egg business. And Charles Lewis built his magnificent showplace farm east of the village. To the south, Paul Myers cleared thirty acres of Killdeer woods and killed as many rattlers in the process. "You learned to smell 'em," he said. "And you by God tipped a wheat shock over before you forked it on the wagon. Weren't safe on a tractor either. The snakes would strike the tires, get their fangs stuck in the rubber, and as the wheels turned, you'd have rattlers flyin' past your head."

Harpster had its own telephone directory for a while, more marvelous than any communication system today. Calling someone in the area, all we had to do was lift the phone, pressing no infernal buttons, and when Fannie Day intoned, "Number please?" with appropriate pomp and ceremony, ask her the whereabouts of the person we wanted to talk to. She would almost always know, either from other calls or by keeping an eagle eye on the street outside her window. In addition, she would pass on, free of charge, the latest gossip.

But what made Harpster hum, in addition to its farmers (the Wool King, folk history says, once built what was thought to be the largest slatted corn crib in the world) was the railroad with its busy depot, its regular passenger and freight service, and its telegraph. In the thirties and forties, people in Harpster followed a nightly summer ritual: They gathered on porches or in front of the general store, perhaps listening to Herb McBride talk about his Utah sheep ranch, or hear once more how Bob Berline and Bryant Bentley raced barefooted in the snow around and around the store, trying to settle once and for all who could run faster. Then, when the Sportsman roared through at 9:00 P.M., the talkers set their watches and went to bed. No television.

"I made a mistake when television came along," recalled Al Brents. "I got one of the first ones in these parts, a ten-inch $450 Crosley. You wouldn't believe how the people would flock in here to watch the thing. They'd stand in the way of customers and I couldn't budge them. I couldn't sell the damn thing either. Nobody in Harpster was about to pay $450 for something they could watch for free and which might break down at any second. So I raffled it off and got my money out of it. The guy who won it came back twenty years later and said it was still working fine."

There was never a movie theater in Harpster, but Brents got into that action, too. He and other business people sponsored free outdoor movies, with advertisements interspersed between movie reels. Scores of us would flock into town for the free shows—my Uncle Lawrence Rall hauled the kids from our immediate neighborhood in his rickety pickup truck. The man who showed the movies had a projector set up on the back seat of a big Packard, and all he had to do was open the door and turn the thing on, aimed at the screen up against the wall of the fire station next to the railroad tracks. We sat on the ground, on folding chairs brought along, or in the back of trucks, and loudly protested both the advertisements before the show and the villains during it. When the trains rumbled through, the movie had to be stopped until the sound track could be heard again. We accepted these intermissions gracefully, without any realization that we might be the only kids in the world to have our movies interrupted by locomotives.

We all wanted to be train engineers when we grew up.

Harpster pressed its advantage over Little by becoming, in 1916, the site of the new high school and elementary school, beginning the consolidation that would go on to this very day. In our neighborhood, Eagle School was closed, where so many successful people I knew had gotten their education, including longtime Ohio state senator Fritz Cassel and Carl Karcher, who earned fame and fortune in California with his West Coast string of Carl's Jr. fast food restaurants. (Both are still alive today, 1997, as I write.) Also closed was Howalt School, where my father and three of his brothers received their earliest and, they insisted, best education. Uncle Dick eventually became head of the Library Science Department at Columbia University. "Ezra Hall, our teacher at Howalt, was a genius," he said. "I've always called that school Howalt University."

Harpster was so proud to have the new consolidated school

that the farmer-heirs of the fertile pioneer fields, some of them the equivalent of landed gentry, dug deep into their pockets to pay for it. When still more money was needed, Iva Bones and Sarah Sears anted up the balance. Everyone believed with almost religious conviction that in education lay financial success, even though most of them had gained such success after attending only the little red-brick schoolhouses or receiving no formal education at all.

Harpster couldn't foresee that if economic "fate" made consolidation inevitable, then it would not stop at the closing of the one-room schoolhouses. Harpster therefore built its consolidated brick school building to last forever. Had the people been told in 1916 that forever would last only seventy-four years, they would have laughed in disbelief, just as people in Upper Sandusky laugh today at the idea that if "economic fate" continued on its course, their school would be consolidated into that of a more populated town someday too.

Behind the school, Charles Lewis donated land for a park and hired WPA workers to landscape it. This gem of horticultural splendor with its Victorian reflecting pool, enlarged to serve as a wading pool for children, seemed as delightfully out of place in a cornbelt village of 1935 as finding a miniature Taj Mahal there. In the 1940s, on the Fourth of July, which we called "Al Brents Night" because he, along with Paul Myers and Homer Woods, footed most of the bill, hundreds jammed into the park to watch the fireworks. We thought these annual events, too, would go on forever.

In summer my mother would drive my sisters and me from our farm to the park to splash in the pool while she read. Often, we had the lovely place entirely to ourselves. "Like rich people on their estates," Mom would say with a little smile.

In recent years, the village filled the pond with dirt with the publicized intention of making a flower garden on it. The real reason for the change was to discourage drinking parties ("and other scandals," people said darkly) during which the pool became a receptacle for beer cans. Some of the loveliest original plantings in the park died and were not replaced. There was no pool and no flower garden in its place, but the beer cans continued to roll restlessly on the ground. In their graves, David Harpster and Charles Lewis surely rolled restlessly too.

After the school closing, the villagers and farmers fell into a bitter silence of forced acceptance. Sometimes the older ones fondly recalled the last day of school in the old days, when the whole community halted work on farms and in shops, coming by foot, car, buggy, or farm wagon to the school grounds to share a picnic with the students and show their solidarity and commitment for what they thought was their school. Now that they understood it belonged to the state of Ohio, to do with as it wished, many of them, like me, vowed never to vote for a school tax again.

Rosann Binau, my sister, summed up the mood in her newspaper column in the Carey *Progressor Times*:

> [T]he sickening feeling I get when I drive through Harpster, past the school building that sits empty . . . is . . . not a rush of sadness at seeing the dark, blank windows and deserted playground. . . . No, the feeling that turns my stomach starts in my mind. It is from there that it socks downward like a fist. It is a kind of despair, born of the realization that this vacancy was not caused, as it were, by attrition, but was the result of a deliberate policy. . . . I get angry . . . because right there in bricks and mortar is our monument to the shortsighted and unenlightened value system that we as a society seem prone to keep opting for, even if it works, eventually, to our detriment.

But I came to believe that the village would outlive even this tragedy. As I watched and wondered, I saw something optimistic happening: People coming home. Sara (Myers) Gier came home, bringing a husband who, with their sons Jamie and Scot, kept expanding their amazing smithy and artistic metal-working business. Craig Bowman's two sons, Kyle and Steve, came home (from Florida) with their families, to build new homes and take over the farm operation. Tony Arnold came home, an optometrist now, and built a new home on the edge of town across the road from the old Arnold family homestead that his two uncles still farmed. Kay Kenan, Craig's sister, came home (from North Carolina) in her retirement, as Fern Erickson, had done, to live in a new home on the edge of the village. *There is in fact someone always coming home.* The village is growing the way all good growth should come: slowly, almost imperceptibly. Could it be that America is on the verge of a rural rebirth and villages are about to rise again to the homey grandeur they once enjoyed?

CHAPTER *17 /* *A Solitary Farmer Goes to a Rock Concert*

By the odd circumstances that marriage unwittingly arranged, I became personally acquainted with the Damn Yankees, a recently popular rock group. Invited to one of its concerts, I thought it prudent to work up slowly to the experience by going to a Jimmy Buffett concert first. Sort of like training for a drinking bout by starting on wine coolers and graduating, sip by sip, up to boilermakers. The cultural shock might otherwise prove fatal to someone who lived in the woods and thought the cawing of a crow was unseemly loud.

But I'm getting ahead of my story. Actually, what happened first was that a friend, Steve, caught me in an unguarded moment as I listened contentedly to the sweet song of a meadowlark drifting across my pasture field.

"Have you ever been to a rock concert?"

"A rock concert?" I answered suspiciously. "What's that?"

"Well, what I have in mind is not exactly a rock concert. How would you like to go to a Jimmy Buffett concert?"

"Who's Jimmy Buffett?"

And so it came to pass that I could eventually answer both questions with some authority. A rock concert was what happened when you dropped a hound dog into a barrel with three raccoons and clamped the lid down tight. A not-quite-rock Jimmy Buffett concert was an ordeal where you stood for three hours on a folding chair at Beulah Park in Columbus, Ohio, dodging beach balls and trying to keep from getting beer spilled all over you, compliments of other people around you also standing on folding chairs, dodging beach balls.

There was probably more to it than that, but on my first adventure into the land of ear-splitting sound decibels, I could not hear the songs that Jimmy Buffett was executing (an apt word) at what seemed like several miles away on the stage because everyone around me was trying to execute the songs along with Buffett, meanwhile amusing themselves by keeping various balloon shapes, including inflated condoms, flying above the throng. Buffett himself was visible only for brief seconds when the couple in front of me, standing on their folding chairs of course, swayed apart far enough in their lovemaking for me to focus my birdwatching binoculars on the stage. Only because of long experience at sighting Blackburnian warblers high in treetops was I able to spot Buffett at all in those fleeting moments, and then I was not sure which one of the seemingly crazed performers up there, flitting like moths in and out of the stage lights and pumping iron with guitars—once even with a harmonica—really was him. But even in the seconds when someone who might have been Jimmy Buffett was visible on the stage, I found myself distracted by the lovers coming to grips with reality in front of me again. That scene should not necessarily have been distracting to a denizen of the barnyard except that the female of the species, in tune with rock concert fashion, was wearing only a few calculated scraps of see-through fabric in place of conventional clothing.

The other reason that I was predisposed to go to a real rock concert in spite of the music was Steve's parrot hat. I quickly learned that the parrot is to Buffettland what the white cow is to India. To be called a parrothead is the highest compliment. To own a hat shaped like a parrot is every parrothead's dream. Steve's hat was made of plastic foam, and he would not tell anyone where he had gotten it because it had magical power. On my bald head, it transformed me into an object of intrigue and/or desire to scores of admiring men and lovely women who happened by. Where had Steve found such a hat? Would he sell it? Name his price. Two girls hinted not too subtly that they would do almost anything for a chance to wear it the rest of the evening. That's when Steve demanded his hat back.

If this happened at a relatively laid-back Buffett concert, what would happen at a real rock concert, I wondered.

I eventually figured out that the game the parrotheads were playing was to see who could first recognize the next song emanating from the stage several miles away and then respond the quickest with the proper fetish or cultural ritual that by common consent went with the song. Buffett had but to stroke one chord on his guitar, or have a stagehand switch on a certain purple flood light, or the drummer jerk the right muscle, and in that crowd of 15,000 people, 14,999 responded on cue: shouted the appropriate *damn*, *hell*, or *fuck*, did the right jig, threw balloon imitations of sharks or Margarita bottles into the air, or made weird motions with their hands like the celebrant intoning the gospel reading at a Catholic High Mass.

That was an apt simile. Although the people seemed bent on showing each other that they were just having a good time and mellowing out on beer and Buffett's notion of how a dolphin would sing country-western if it took a notion to do so, they were really practicing their religion. Or unreligion. When Buffett sang what Steve said was the margarita song, the crowd reacted in approximately the same way that a church full of aging Episcopalians reacts to "Nearer My God to Thee." In fact, Buffett came on stage at one point wearing what I would have sworn was a chasuble and did a takeoff on traditional forms of religion that drove the audience to hysterics. "If we weren't all crazy, we would go insane," they chanted along with Buffett.

The parrotheads did not really get drunk on all the cheap beer they were drinking, I noted, but pretended a quasi-drunkenness in order to disguise or excuse the fervency of their sacred reverence for Buffett music, margaritas, and parrots. I did not encounter one mean person, and despite all the beer, there were no fights or even scuffles except when Steve tried to get his parrot hat back.

After the concert, I told Steve that "Margaritaville" had whetted my appetite for harder stuff and that I was now going to a concert by the Damn Yankees. His eyes widened in horror.

"You're not ready for that," he said. "You don't even own a black leather jacket."

"Well, can't I just wear your parrot hat?"

"You won't need it."

So back to Beulah Park I journeyed, to pursue the meaning of the Throng. A veteran now, I took along a towel to wipe beer off my chair in case I had to sit down. But Damn Yankee fans did not stand on their chairs and spill beer. They stood on the ground and waved fists clenched so tight that a swizzle stick would not have fit inside them, much less a cardboard tankard of beer.

Not that it mattered because I was now in row 1 thanks to my connection with the Damn Yankees. There was nothing between me and the stage except about ten trillion decibels of noise emanating from a wall of speakers as high as my hay loft.

Were those frantic men on the stage the same Ted Nugent, Tommy Shaw, Jack Blade, and Michael Cartellone I thought I was acquainted with? In the real world, I had found them to be gentlemanly, mature, friendly almost to a fault, family-oriented, and even, with the exception of Ted, subdued. Now, apparently berserk, although they told me that they shunned drugs and drank very little, the four pranced and danced upon the stage like a bunch of calves turned out on pasture the first time in spring. They were screaming out their hit song "Coming of Age." I bowed my head, shoved a finger in each ear, and awaited death by sonar ray, like in those old Flash Gordon epics. I was old enough to have fathered Ted Nugent, who was no spring chicken, and it occurred to me that here in the final moments of my life, *I* was the one "coming of age," not all those stomping, arm-flailing, young people in the audience. I jammed in the ear plugs that Carol had brought along—the kind swimmers wear—but they were useless. Although my ears had been permanently damaged at age eleven by driving a mufflerless tractor day after day, standing twenty feet away from one of the loudest sound systems in the world was still an awesome, mind-blotting, physically painful experience—an eclipse of intellect as well as an extinction of eardrums. One of the guards in front of the stage, seeing my predicament, stepped forward and gave me waxed-sponge plugs like he was wearing. With them in place, I could actually hear some of the individual words and notes.

The noise did not much bother my eyes, however, and so close to the performers, I was dumbstruck by the awesome physical energy that the four performers poured into their work and the total lack of rationality that they exhibited. I tried to remember how I had first met Nugent, now riding his guitar around the stage like a witch on a broomstick. Ted had been sitting backstage holding his baby daughter, arm around his wife, sipping *water*, a far, far cry from the Motor City Madman he became on stage. What Ted wanted to talk about then was the blessed solitude and peace of his thousand acres of farm and forest in Michigan. There, at least, *there on my land*, he had said, wildness and solitude would reign as long as he lived. Realizing that I was, in a strange way, a spiritual brother to the real Ted Nugent even though I despised rock music, I wanted to ask him if he might not, deep down, despise it too. But I was afraid to. Afraid that I would learn that he really did like it.

Cartellone on stage, glistening with sweat rolling down his naked torso, periodically breaking hickory drumsticks over his drums and tossing the pieces to the crowd, was not the Cartellone I remembered sitting quietly with his mother, teasing her gently about the coarse language of the concert. Who would ever guess, now, as he broke a brass cymbal at the orgiastic climax of a song, that he enjoyed quieter kinds of music too, and that he was a talented painter in oils and watercolor. "I am fulfilled by my work," he once said to me. "I don't need chemicals to feel alive." But now it was another world full of people who needed, if not chemicals, the chemicaloid noise of rock to feel alive. The music boomed and the performers shrieked, leaped, slid, tumbled, jerked, and rolled spasmodically around the stage, exactly—*exactly*—like the Holy Rollers who had so frightened me as a child when they tumbled out the door of their storefront church uptown in a frenzy of religious hysteria. The fans screamed applause and tried to imitate the performers in the cramped space between the rows of seats— dancing, prancing, clomping, stomping, thumping, humping, and pounding the air with fists. The heavy beat blotted out all hearing of the music, rose up out of the floor, growing like some reptilian vine up the agitated legs and into the yearning groins of the audience. I could feel it myself, a visceral explosion sending these people into a frenzied yet pathetically passive animal pursuit of an aliveness that they did not realize must originate within a person, not from without, if it is to be possessed. They kept extending their arms toward the stage, reaching out, reaching out for more. More of what?

I felt intellect slipping away. I tried to fix my attention on a little white hole in my mind through which I could see beyond this enclosed whirlpool of noise into a faraway place where meadowlarks sang. What drove all these people to turn their backs on meadowlark song in favor of sonar, electronic pulsations? I now began to see what Claudia Roth Pierpont must have meant (in the August 20, 1990, *New Yorker*): "Today's notions of artistic purity rest on the airy, romantic premise that words give out where music begins, that language cedes its power in deference to music, because *music* is the more articulate, the more profound." Yes, indeed. When it came to rock music at least, words failed. But more profoundly, even with barnyard music, the music of animal herds, which sometimes reminds me of rock and roll, "language cedes its power in deference to music."

That was what I was about to learn, for the end of the concert was not the real end of the concert. That came as the Throng filed out the exit corridor. As fifteen thousand people tried to work through the narrow exit, literal gridlock occurred. The people in front slowed to barely a crawl while the crowd in back pressed ever forward. Bodies squeezed together so tightly that individual space and action become impossible. A human traffic jam. The mass of people quickly congealed into one huge beast whose name was Throng. For the individual, there was no stopping, no turning back, no speeding up, no place to turn aside—the worst level of Hell that a solitary farmer could experience. A child or old person, falling, would have been trampled. An electric tremor of uneasiness flashed through the bodies globbed together like maggots in carrion. I thought of how a colony of sawfly larvae, alarmed, all raised their heads from their eating in unison to resemble a pulsating wave of hairs standing on end. I could feel the anxiety surging through Throng, and saw that feeling reflected in the eyes of people around me. Little flashes of pushing and shoving and angry words broke out as the people behind continued to press forward when there was no forward to gain. I had the sinking fear that with even the slightest provocation, Throng might turn violent and whip its tail like a dragon, mashing bodies into human hamburger through the iron grillwork that flanked the sides of the exit corridor.

But from somewhere behind me came a human voice, *bellowing like a cow*. Throng trembled with laughter. Bawling cow noises now arose from different places. The idea caught on. Sheep blattings joined in the chorus. Then some donkey-like hee-haws. A concert of barnyard music filled the air. Intellect had realized that Throng was dangerously like a herd of cattle. To protect itself, to transcend animality, intellect was aping animality.

Tension drained from the air. I had a sudden illumination: That's what rock concerts were really about. The sounds of animality relieving the tensions of modern life. I smiled for the first time in hours. There was hope after all. From afar I thought I heard a meadowlark.

CHAPTER 18/ *You Can Step into the Same Haystack Twice*

I adhere to the droll theory that haystacks were invented to give lovers a cozy place to snuggle down in and watch the fireflies mingle with the stars on a peaceful midsummer's night. According to this theory, only later did farmers discover that haystacks were a good way to store grass for livestock too. But love was not the main reason I decided to build a haystack again, at least not that kind of love. I realized that my grandson, Evan, paging through a book about the kind of farms that no longer existed, didn't have the foggiest notion of what sliding down a haystack was all about or, by extension, could he understand very much about his land-rooted culture. The eloquently grim meaning of a biblical warning like "He shall come down like rain on mown grass" was wholly lost on him. Nor could he appreciate the significance of "trying to find a needle in a haystack" or "making hay while the sun shines." Reading his nursery rhymes, he could not come close to imagining a time when Little Boy Blue was *real*, when children his age could contribute to a family's economic life by looking after the sheep and at the same time be so blessedly free of adult supervision.

So I decided to build a haystack, something not seen in our neighborhood since my grandfather quit farming about 1944. But how? Although haystacks were still being made in some parts of the world, even in the western United States, I could find no one doing so in Ohio, where agrifactories, landfill mountains, nuclear power plants, waste incinerators, and empty beer cans graced the rural landscape. My friend John Fichtner, who farmed in West Virginia, was the closest husbandman I knew who was contrary enough, like me, to build haystacks. Were there any secrets to it? Well, yes, he knew one. Traditionally, a pole was set up first and the hay stacked around it. The pole acted like a stabilizer to keep the stack from toppling over after the livestock started eating into it.

So after selecting a protected but well-drained spot in the field closest to the barn, I first planted a pole, a straight honey locust sapling that I had been wanting to cut down anyway.

Evan got the whole show. He watched me mow the hay down and rake it into windrows. When the hay was dry, I hauled it to the site where the stack was to be built. In Grandpaw's day, the hay was picked up out of the windrow with what we called a buck rake or buck-Ford, since it was usually a huge wooden scoop that fit on the back or front of a remodeled Ford pickup truck. Dad would drive the buck-Ford at breakneck speed down the windrow and scoop up a big jag of hay, then zoom off to the stack, where the hay was deposited on a stacker. The stacker in turn would lift the hay up onto the stack where Grandpaw stood, brandishing his fork like a minuteman his rifle. He would place the hay by careful forkfuls around the perimeter of the mounting pile. When the mechanical stacker could reach no higher, he topped off the stack with a rounded cap of hay that shed water almost as well as a canvas.

Without either a buck-Ford or a stacker, I used the hydraulic manure fork on the front of the tractor to do the work of both. Jerry, my son, built a big wooden scoop to fit over the steel manure tines and we were in business. The scoop would pick up a jag of about five hundred pounds of hay out of the windrow fairly well, then I'd drive the tractor to the stack, and then the hydraulic system would raise the scoopful high enough to build, by increments, a stack about 15 feet tall—small by traditional standards. Since I had never built a stack before, but knew considerable skill was required, I set up a ring of woven-wire fence about fifteen feet in diameter to start the stack and dumped the hay evenly around the circle. That assured me that the first five feet of stack would be more or less perfectly vertical. Once above that, I could still use the raised scoop to stack hay into a vertical wall 15 feet high before topping off with a cap to shed water.

The stack went up fairly easily. Its sides did not rise as phallically vertical as Grandpaw's used to, but it did shed water reasonably well. In early winter, when pasture ran out, I removed the woven-wire fence from around the stack. The sheep had already been reaching through it to pull out hay, and now they and the cows snuggled around the stack when the wintry winds blew and ate with gusto. In short order the stack began to take the shape of a toadstool with a fat stem, just as I remembered from my boyhood. And sure enough, the stack slid slowly down the pole without toppling over as the animals ate around the bottom.

What had begun as a whim I now saw was an extremely practical idea. I had not had to buy anything to store and feed hay in this manner. Using the loader to build it reduced the labor of hauling and handling the hay into the barn mow by more than half. The cost of renting or buying a baler, which I could hardly justify for the small amount of hay I put up each year, was avoided. The stacked hay cured better and with a much better aroma than hay cured in the bale. There was surprisingly little wasted hay— maybe eight inches on the bottom and four inches on the top and that was not really wasted because it became in the following year a splendid mulch bed for growing melons in, as Grandpaw always did. The animals could feed themselves from the stack without my help. My only job was to rearrange the board gates I put around the stack as it diminished so that sheep and especially the cows would not trample more than they ate.

Why had haystacks gone out of style for small farms? There was nothing obsolete about them. In fact, with the advent of the front-end loader for tractors, haystacks became extremely practical and modern. Hay was my biggest expense if I had to buy it, and the loader and the stack gave me a cheap way to make it. I had raised a monument not to the past as I intended, but to the continuing wisdom of tradition. Haystacks would become a part of our farm's landscape again.

Our old milk cow ate holes in the side of the stack big enough to envelope her whole head, neck, and shoulders, just as I remembered from long ago. Evan and I crawled back into these holes, back into the nineteenth century, and stared contentedly out at the raw winds of the twenty-first century blowing toward us over the pasture. And we both understood how hard it was to find even a pocketknife in a haystack, let alone a needle.

CHAPTER *19* / *Living Economically*
Happy Ever After

THE SHEPHERD AND THE CORNHUSKER

Conversation shifted from grumbling about crops and weather to grumbling about making a profit in farming. But you die rich, and then the kids fight over it. Yeah. A pause. Al, my farmer-neighbor eyed me quizzically. I could tell he was trying to work up enough nerve to ask me something personal. Since I farmed only a small amount of land, it was a matter of great curiosity to him how Carol and I made ends meet. Finally, he blurted his question: "I know you write, Gene, but what do you do for a living?"

I often asked myself that question. I was engaged in two of the least profitable enterprises I knew: small-scale farming and independent writing. Of course it was possible to make a lot of money either way. In California, garden-farming enterprises, operated with consummate horticultural and marketing skills, could gross upward of fifty thousand dollars an acre with small plots of specialty crops. And of course, again, writers could make a small fortune if they were very good, very lucky, or very famous. Being none of the above, I continued to mutter to myself: I know you write, Gene, but what do you do for a living?

Another farmer in our neighborhood, Gottlieb, had a philosophy on such matters that affected me greatly. He lived to be well over a hundred years old, was in fact still clubbing groundhogs to death with his cane at age one hundred, as the local paper proudly reported. He led an extremely simple life, and so, even from his little sixty-acre grain and livestock farm, he made enough money for his purposes. A friend and I visited him when he was in his eighties or nineties to record some of his observations for posterity. I asked him why he didn't go ahead and remodel his old farmhouse or at least bring water into the house since I knew he could well afford to. "Oh, that would be too much trouble," he said, dismissing the question with a wave of his hand. "I'll soon be dead anyway." But he kept on living contentedly for many more years, without indoor plumbing. He'd watch the cars zoom by on the new highway and wonder aloud: "Where are all those people trying to go, anyway?" Real estate brokers bugged him to sell his fertile, little, well-tended farm, and his answer always was: "Oh, I guess not. Whatever would I do with the money?"

For much of my life I was poor in money and never more than modestly middle class, but I never felt poor. I never wanted much, except to be free of all bossery. Anybody with the least amount of smarts and determination could make a lot of money, it seemed to me, by riding the coattails of any big company or institution. What was difficult was learning to live well without money.

When we left graduate school, having lived for four years on about $3,600 a year, Carol and I borrowed $25,000 to buy a house and a car. I started working at *Farm Journal* magazine for $9,000 a year and nine years later, when I left, I was making $20,000, not a whole lot of money in 1974 but considerably more than $20,000 would ever be again. Back home, prepared to take any job I could get that would allow me time for writing and farming, I was lucky enough to land a contract from Rodale Press to write magazine articles and books for $16,000 a year. Every year I expected that contract to be discontinued, but instead it increased until by 1982, it paid $28,000 a year. In some of those years, royalties from books added to that income a little.

Then I experienced my only brush with financial success by my standards. My income for about four years soared to the mid-forty thousands from royalties. But all that did was increase my desire to quit mundane how-to journalism in favor of more serious creative writing. So I gave up my contract in 1983 and my income fell slowly but steadily ever after. But my happiness in what I was doing increased. Between contractual assignments, I wrote two novels that no one would publish but the creation of which filled me with great exhilaration. And I completed the first draft of this book.

Over the years, Carol and I averaged about $25,000 a year from all sources—school-teacher wages without the generous health and pension benefits that teachers enjoy. Carol did not work outside the home until our children were teenagers, and then only for three months of the year. She did eventually inherit $15,000. I inherited, from a distant relative, $17.50. But by so-called retirement time we were out of debt, living comfortably enough on about $9,000 worth of Social Security and about $12,000 of earned income, plus a couple thousand dollars of interest income from savings, interest which we were able (so far) to keep in the bank. That probably sounds like a lot of money to some people; a Spartan existence to others. Wealth is a very relative concept. I could point to friends who spent even less money a year than we did and who were quite content and happy. Having always lived modestly, operating small farms or running small businesses, or even working in factories (rather than being imbecilic enough to try to make a living as a minor writer like I did), they had net worth in cash and property far greater than the world at large would think possible, all laid away little by little over the years without blazing off in glory to the city or to college, without any fanfare at all from the world of "success," without ever succumbing to the commercial dragons of over-consumption. Theirs is the greatest success, I think, because they always enjoyed the quiet life of home and did not trade their personal freedom for a big income that demanded total commitment and slavery to the gods of commerce.

People who wanted to go home again began asking me how to make the finances work. I was nonplused. How could I advise anyone on how to make money or the best ways to save it? I just tried not to spend the stuff, even refraining from expenditures that would have been profitable, and put whatever I could in the safest investments the bank offered, avoiding all those lucrative schemes in stocks and bonds that might have meant a securer old age for us. I tried not to think about finances. Worrying about money was almost totally debilitating to my writing, which seemed to require an aura of tranquillity around me. My real wealth was that Carol provided that aura.

When I tried to explain to people how we made ends meet, I tended to fall back on old clichés which I found amazingly correct if not pressed too hard.

"The love of money is the root of all evil."

"Never spend more in a month than you make in a week." A farmer I worked for once was fond of saying that. He was quite wealthy, although he seemed to enjoy living very frugally. His daughter, age twenty, who already had plenty of money of her own from working hard on their farm, bought clothes at the Goodwill store and altered them to fit her attractively. When she wanted a rowboat for fishing, she never considered buying one. She found an old, sunken hulk along a lake with the floor rotted out and rebuilt it. Last time I talked to her, she said she had run across one of my books—while vacationing in Europe.

"Neither a borrower nor a lender be." From Shakespeare, though hardly original with him. Borrowing for a house to live in usually paid off because of inflation of property values, but that was partly an illusion. With interest payments I noticed that I would pay for the house twice over the period of the mortgage. The only advantage was that the interest payments were deductible from income taxes. Be that as it may, I decided that borrowing for anything that decreased in value, like a car, was horribly poor home economics, and we pinched and saved till we could escape that trap. Over a lifetime, transportation costs could easily exceed housing costs, mostly to go places I didn't want to go.

"Mark well the pennies, and the dollars will take care of themselves."

"Do in life the work you love, and love will find a way to make it pay." I wish I could remember where I read that. It was an observation that became not only true for me in general but sometimes true in specific instances that I did not hesitate to call miraculous, since for me, God was literally the power of love that flows between people. One year when our finances were particularly tight, I received a letter out of the blue from a faraway, total stranger. With no strings attached at all, with only the vaguest explanation that something I had written touched his heart, this unknown benefactor gifted me $1200 right when I needed it badly. On other occasions, a certain editor continued to buy articles from me, I was sure, because he knew I needed the money. He certainly did not need my contributions.

"Buy low; sell high." This truism had a special significance for me. It always appeared to me that for poorer people who would sacrifice to save a little money every day, inflation was a great economic boon: such a person could take advantage of it when selling but avoid it when buying. This seemed to be one of the keys to Amish economics which enormously influenced me. These people were successful in business because they lived partially in the nineteenth century, but sold their products in the twentieth. In our case, the price of our home in Philadelphia doubled by the time we sold it, which was the only reason we could build a new house back home. Our new house in the rural boondocks cost us half of what it would have cost in Philadelphia. Also, "buy low and sell high" in a relative sense was the secret to my ability to stay afloat financially. The overhead of putting words on paper cost almost nothing except for the time involved, which I did not value in money but as a precious opportunity to follow my own heart. No matter how cheaply I sold my words, and sometimes that was below minimum wage on an hourly basis, I was making a huge percent of profit over out-of-pocket costs. Brain power was virtually free.

Beyond owning a newer car, we avoided outstanding expenses as a matter of course. Health insurance, however, was a heavy burden for us when we were self-employed and could not find a group plan to enroll in. I noticed, angrily, how that situation was becoming a major obstacle for small home businesses, and I wondered if there were not some malice in the way big business and big labor kept "group insurance" out of our reach. Could it have been that big business and big labor, not to mention big government, disliked home businesses? That kind of independence made totalitarian power nervous and was difficult to collect taxes from. But we were blessed with good health and so at least never had hospital bills beyond insurance coverage.

We never took what could be called a real vacation, although we enjoyed short, cheap trips through the year visiting family and friends. Our only real extravagances were eating out in quality restaurants, which we enjoyed at least twice a month, and sponsoring our softball team. We didn't play golf, bowl, suck constantly on beer or soft drink cans in lieu of drinking water, go to movies, professional sports or musical events. The Damn Yankees concert (see chapter 17) was certainly enough to last me a lifetime. We did not invest in expensive wardrobes and owned only a little good furniture, although I believed good furniture was a smart investment, not an extravagance, if only I could have afforded it. My cheap suits lasted fifteen years because I wore them so infrequently. Same with my "good" shoes. We did buy expensive work shoes regularly after learning that cheap ones harmed not only our feet but backs and legs as well.

The only apparent downside to our rather modest income level was that I had to keep on working in retirement. But I liked what I was doing and wouldn't quit even if I were a billionaire. In fact, with "retirement" I could finally turn down the purely commercial writing I found boring and concentrate on more creative if less profitable possibilities. The result was that I was busier than ever, albeit for even less money. The neat thing, however, was that at any time, even in my so-called dotage, I might finally write something wonderful and make some real money.

Perhaps not so strangely, this situation was true also in the case of our farming. Instead of being forced to try to make a business profit from it, in time we could focus on creative, adventuresome projects: developing a practical, open-pollinated corn with extremely large ears for faster handhusking, at which I was having some success; perfecting nearly year-round grazing with sheep, which was coming along nicely; and finding practical methods of backyard aquaculture, which was also proving practical. I was also interested in making ethanol (legal moonshine) and soybean oil for small-tractor fuel, making medicines from herbs, and breeding miniature cows for backyard milk production. I could think of a hundred such projects awaiting closer attention: the potential technologies for backyard food production, which I believed would become crucially important in the next century, were only now being envisioned. All these challenges were more interesting than making money, but might, in time, become very profitable in a Wendell Berry, home economics sort of way.

In our first years back home, I planned to shape our little farm into a marketplace for berries, vegetables, flowers, and nursery trees, including Christmas trees, and thereby make about five thousand dollars of our income. I thought I could make another ten thousand writing, and in the typical way that everyone judges financial needs by the current level of inflation, I thought fifteen thousand dollars would be enough. To that goal, we immediately began setting out evergreens, raspberries, strawberries, and asparagus to go along with annual crops of sweet corn, tomatoes, muskmelons, and flowers. Based on our experiences on the two acres outside Philadelphia, these were the crops that would be the most profitable with the least risk. Subsequent experience supported that assumption, except maybe for raspberries, which were a big gamble, to be undertaken seriously only by those who could stand to take a loss in some years. In fact, these crops turned out to be even more practical as time went by, considering the connections that we continued to make with local people and restaurants yearning to get fresh garden produce.

But every year, demand for my writing kept taking more time, not less, and pressed by our modest income, I dared not turn the work down although I often wished to. I heeded advice attributed to Yogi Berra: "When you come to a fork in the road, take it." I kept on writing, writing, writing, and I kept experimenting, experimenting, experimenting on the farm with various projects that could be handled properly in spare time and might be turned into significant cash income quickly in case my word production suffered a crop failure.

In our farming, we were extremely tight with money. One tractor was a 1950 model, which cost me only $200 plus $1,500 for restoration. The other, a 1967 model, cost me $7,000. Both, in good repair, I could sell for more than I had in them. Actually I don't really need the older tractor anymore but keep it as a modest "luxury." To replace it with a new tractor of the same horsepower would cost me $27,000. My ancient (and obsolete) disk, cultipacker and two harrows I begged from kindly commercial farmers. A newer disk came as part of the deal with the '67 tractor. My manure spreader cost us $100. My two-row cornplanter was two Garden Way seeders, $70 each, bolted to a homemade frame. The old hayrake cost me $15, the sickle bar mower $150, and the rotary mower $200. The hydraulic front-end lift, key to the cheap way I make hay (see chapter 18), came with the '67 tractor and was the reason I bought it. Though old, all these tools continue to run with minor repairs unto this day. For planting grass, clover, and small-grain seeds, I bought a handcranked broadcast spreader for $40. We did, however, invest in a good rotary tiller. If I prorated these costs over the thirty to forty years I expected the machines to last, the annual expense would clearly be quite modest, and at the end of that time, they might have even higher value as antiques.

With writing demands ruling out commercial, time-consuming market gardening, we decided to operate our farm like a traditional grain and livestock family farm of the 1940s, in miniature. I wanted a farming enterprise that could be a model for anyone with another home-based business. But to make so small a farm economically legitimate in the eyes of other farmers and people reading my books, I wanted every acre of the thirty-two we owned, even the woods and scrubbiest pasture land, to show a profit per acre comparable to what large-scale grain farmers in our area were making. At that I became successful most years. If I counted the food we ate at retail price—what we'd have to pay for it in the stores—my profit per acre looked even better.

Yearly income:
Net from lambs, wholesale to stockyards: $1,000
Approximate retail value of one lamb for home consumption: $100
Approximate retail value of meat from 2 hogs: $350
Approximate retail value of meat from one steer: $700
Approximate retail value of meat from 30 broilers: $120
Approximate value of 100 dozen, free-range eggs: $200
Approximate value of 50 quarts of milk/cream saved out for table use: $75.00
Approximate retail value of vegetables and fruits: $400
Estimated net value of 4 cords of hardwood used to replace oil or electric heat: $400
Annual sale of hardwood logs from woodland to date: $225
Value of sawn lumber, less cost of custom bandsawing, per-year to date: $200
Miscellaneous—honey; value of manure replacing fertilizer; value of wild foods consumed, including pond fish, squirrels, berries, and nuts: $50

That amounted to about $3,800 or well over $100 per acre, the goal that we set for ourselves.

Agricultural economists, almost always defensive when faced with positive figures for small farming, pointed out that I was not charging a cost to labor, which was true. I didn't consider my labor a cost but rather a profit, part of my chosen way of life. Furthermore, if I were not laboring on my farm, what would I be doing elsewhere in my spare time that would actually cost money? I asked economists how to set a recreational value on a farm—the money saved by enjoying life there rather than spending money for recreation elsewhere. They didn't seem to know. Farming was a cold hard business; fun did not fit into their commercial frame of reference.

Other costs of food production were extremely low. My machinery mostly depreciated out in short order. Almost all feed for the livestock was homegrown, the greater portion of it harvested by the animals themselves through grazing. I burnt about a hundred gallons of gasoline annually in farm and garden work, plus a few changes of oil and occasional battery replacement. For the sake of proper accounting, I should have figured in a fixed land-cost for owning the property, but I would have that cost whether I farmed the land or not. And would I have charged it to my home writing business or to the farm?

More interesting to the part-time farmer, I thought, was to examine the animal-production figures alone. I devoted only about nine acres of the farm to the sheep, cow and calves, two hogs, and the hens and broilers, about eight in various pasture crops and one in grains. In this scenario, using farm-gate wholesale figures, not retail figures, the profit picture looked like this:

> Net from lambs: $1,100
> Net from 2 market hogs bought as $40 feeder pigs: $100
> Net from one 800-lb. beef: $300
> Net from free-range broilers and eggs: $180
> Net from about 3 months of milk at farm-gate price: $24.00

That came to a total of about $1,700 from nine acres, which was getting close to $200 per acre net. In contrast, the large-scale commercial grain farmer had so much out-of-pocket cost per acre, especially if he hired most of the labor, that he was lucky to net $30 an acre most years. I was mystified at how economists could insist that such large-scale farming was more "efficient" than small-scale farming. The larger farms made more total money, of course, but were far less efficient per acre. As my tiny farm continued to improve in managed rotational grazing, the figures would only get better, I hoped, and presumably my management ability would too, so that a net of over $200 per acre was distinctly possible if I didn't count my labor as a cost. Since my methods could be used on up to forty acres (probably more than that), still as a part-time venture, the net income could be, for that many acres, $8,000. When the economists quibbled with my numbers, being unable to imagine any economic frame of reference other than their own, I assumed for the sake of argument that I was only two-thirds right and one-third hot air. That still came to $6,000 net for a rather lovely sideline business, a figure that could rise much higher as small-scale technologies improved.

Although I thought my figures were legitimate enough, I was much opposed to using them, to aping the precious way economists clung to their calculations. First of all, because of the way accountants legitimately figure costs for tax purposes, I could show a loss most years as a commercial business just as so many commercial farmers did. Furthermore, there was a far cry between the realities of farming and the cold rigidity of numbers. In a deeper sense, I was not comfortable with the whole economic vogue of using numbers at all to prove the dollar legitimacy of garden farming. My goal was to remove backyard food-production from dollar economics. My values, my frame of reference, and my definitions were different. I could, of course, not escape mainstream economics. Not even monks, holed up in a monastery and following a vow of poverty, could entirely divorce themselves from dollar economics. But my intent was, as far as humanly possible, to separate home food-production from the ratiocinations of supply and demand, manipulation and subsidy, profit and loss, speculation and bargaining. In my frame of reference, land was not a commodity to be bought and sold but civilization's source of sustenance to be held in trust. Time was not money, but the occasion to maintain that trust. Money was not a tool of totalitarian power, but the symbol of faith between humans, just as God was the symbol of love between humans. In such a world, arguing about "efficiency" in the usual sense was ludicrous.

So, as the numbers dictated, I became a shepherd. But I did

not do so because of the numbers. The numbers worked out that way because I discovered that I liked to raise sheep. I saw them as a good way to achieve the main purpose of my very small-scale farming, which was to show how a garden-farm like ours might be a model for a network of such homesteads, building a strong, economically stable and ecologically healthy community. Sheep fit my situation and, more importantly, my temperament. I *liked* the poor dumb things. Watching lambs gamboling across the pasture was a tremendous profit in my accounting ledger, not expressible in prosaic economic terms.

But practically, sheep fit too. They could glean a livelihood from pastures too hilly for sustainable cultivation. On good level farmland, on a small scale, they could make more money per acre from pasture than erosive and chemically sprayed grain. Sheep could provide both meat and milk if one wanted both; produced wool, a most durable and practical fabric for clothing and carpets; gave excellent weed control in rotated crops while reducing herbicides or avoiding them altogether; required little time except during lambing; and were easier to handle and fence than cattle. I could net at least $100 per acre on a small acreage and a small number of sheep, if I did not count my labor as a cost, selling lambs on the open market. The potential for increasing that profit while increasing soil fertility was somewhat open-ended. What if market wool prices rose to profitable levels again? What if the lambs were sold retail to private customers above the open market price? What if the flock were managed as a dairy business, selling the milk for processing into cheeses, as a few homesteaders were doing? What if the wool were processed, spun, and woven into clothing and fabrics, as a great many more homesteaders were doing?

Sheep could be raised healthfully with only a small percentage of the farm in annual cultivated crops. That meant farming without much expense for machinery, chemicals, and fertilizer, and reducing erosion almost entirely. The sheep did most of the harvesting by grazing and left their manure and urine for fertilizer.

The amount of corn I needed to supplement pasturage and hay was so small I could plant and harvest it by hand.

In a managed grazing program, sheep were better for me than full-sized cattle because I could graze them longer in the fall and earlier in the spring. On our clay ground, heavier animals would make footprints six inches deep when the sod was soft from winter rains or spring thaws. (This was why the new miniature Bellfair dairy cow could be an even better alternative than sheep, given the American preference for beef and cow's milk to lamb and ewe's milk. The Bellfair could be grazed like sheep.)

Again because of size, it was easier, safer, and cheaper to keep a ram or two than a bull. I'd been bruised by rams, but bulls could kill. (Another plus for the miniature Bellfairs.)

Sheep manure was easier to handle than cow manure. Less bedding was needed in the barn to keep sheep pens dry and clean than cow stanchions. On the pasture, the sheep pellets did not tend to cover the grass the way cow droppings did, and did not need to be mechanically scattered out.

Actually our sheep preferred to sleep outside on new snow rather than in the barn on cold winter nights. As the old fable said it so well, all a sheep needed was a bite of grass, a pinch of salt, and a sip of water. All else was required not by the animals but by fussy, fastidious, neophyte shepherds.

But I came home to become a shepherd in another way, also unanticipated. I became a shepherd of homesick humans. I had always seen in the "Little Bo Peep" nursery rhyme more than the literal meaning of the lines: "Leave them alone, and they will come home, bringing their tails behind them." I thought that admonition applied to people in more cases than to sheep, and it certainly had applied to me. From the mail and phone calls I was receiving in mounting numbers, it was obvious that most people were trying to come home, if not literally then to someplace they could make into a true home, a place where they actually lived their lives. Some went home not exactly willingly at first, forced to do so by downsizing, and found that losing their high-paying jobs turned out to be a blessing. Some waited until they retired, when they could escape the mad manacles of wage-slavocracy. Some waited until the very end and came home in coffins.

Becoming a shepherd of lost souls was unnerving for me. I was a lost soul myself. But I tried to answer all the questions of the homesick; replied to all their mail; allowed them to come here even when I doubted that visiting me was going to help their troubled spirits; wrote books that I hoped would inspire those with a true vocation for this kind of living and would discourage those who were only fantasizing. I became a shepherd, calling home those people who should never have left in the first place. How much profit per acre is this worth in accounting terms?

◻

In time, I accepted Noble Goodman's invitation to get into the cornhusking contests. By strange coincidence, the field where the contests took place bordered what had once been my grandfather's farm. I could look up from rows of corn and see the woodlot where my father and I had spent tranquil noondays eating lunch during corn harvest, hunting squirrels, or just talking. A rich man's large mansion stood among those trees now, right where there had once lain a circle of stones. During my craze for gathering rocks for a house I thought I was going to build, I suggested to Dad that I haul away those stones. He was silent with disapproval, and I thought it was because my idea of house-building was so impractical. But then he explained. He and Mom had placed the rocks in the circle, he said. "Your mother and I often picnicked there. That's where I proposed to her." He didn't want his little shrine moved.

So now as I took my stand in the corn row, to see how much I could husk in a half hour, to join the age-old dance of the corn harvest and become a part of the unbroken flow of human time,

I could look up on the horizon and see the place where, in a sense, my life began.

That I could see on the horizon something of personal significance was not that strange, I realized. If the whole county were covered with fresh snow and all the tracks of my wanderings over it were imprinted there, almost every section of land in any of the thirteen townships would show my trails. In some places, my crisscrossing footsteps would be so numerous as to pack the snow solid. The eight hundred–some miles of roadways in the county I had also traveled many times. Along every trail and every road were places where little events important to me had happened—trysting places, tiny adventures that shaped or influenced my life in some small or large way. This was home, and it was so vast and deep and high and wide that I could never tire of it.

So now, my turn came to husk. Junior Frey brought his wagon and horses alongside as I slipped on my husking peg. The checker moved in behind me with a sack to garner any ears I missed and deduct their weight from the weight of my husking. Carol stood beside me, as always, ready to cheer me on. Marilyn, my sister, was there too, that "boy-did-we-have-fun" look as bright on her face as it had been fifty-five years ago. "Go!" the timer roared, and I began husking, fumbling at first, then slipping into the smooth, rocking step of a cornhusker moving from stalk to stalk down the row. At first I was laughing. This was supposed to be only a loving reenactment of the past. But soon I felt a more compelling reason for my efforts. There were young people watching my hands closely, and I wanted them to know that I did this not just for a sentimental contest, but in my own cornfield every year. I did it because this was the most economical way to harvest corn on a garden-farm. I did it today. I would be doing it tomorrow. Until infirmity stopped me. As my momentum increased, I seemed to break some barrier of time. I was all alone then, just myself and a team of horses and a cornfield. Hands and husking peg assumed a life of their own, the peg slashing through the husk at the base of the ear, left hand enclosing the loosened husk at the same time, right hand grabbing the bared ear, snapping it free, tossing it into the wagon, one fluid motion, my eyes already glancing ahead for the next ear. A transcendent peace filled me. It was 1940 again. Or maybe eternity. Heraclitus was wrong: Water flowed to the sea, evaporated into the sky, and fell as rain back on the land to flow again. Time, like water, could be defined, as the philosophers said, only as "now flowing." I had come home all the way. I had learned how to step into the same river twice.